THE

WEIGHT

TRAINING

WORKBOOK

BY JIM BENNETT
INTRODUCTION BY BILL PEARL
2ND EDITION

- THE BASICS OF WEIGHT TRAINING
- ABDOMINAL EXERCISES
- CHEST EXERCISES
- TRICEP EXERCISES
- BICEP EXERCISES
- FOREARM EXERCISES
- BACK EXERCISES
- SHOULDER EXERCISES
- LEG EXERCISES
- CALF EXERCISES
- WEIGHT TRAINING RECORDS

Illustrations by Tom Yessis, Patty Blackburn, Jim Furnner
and David Kacmarynski

Published by JBBA Publishing, a Division of JBBA, Inc.
Post Office Box 842
Appleton, Wisconsin 54912-0842
800-245-7897

Manufactured in the United States of America
Printed by Bang Printing

ISBN: 1-879031-06-X

AOL Screen Name: JBBA7897

O my strength, I will sing praises to Thee;
For God is my stronghold, the God who shows me lovingkindness.
Psalm 59:17 NAS

CONTENTS

INTRODUCTION
by Bill Pearl

Every year more and more weight training books hit the shelves with a life-span of the first printing and then vanish into obscurity. The reasons for the lack of success of these books are as numerous as the books themselves.

One of the main reasons for this high attrition rate is that the author banks the success of his or her book on the assumption that everyone wants to look like the bodybuilders seen throughout the book. Nothing could be further from the truth.

With such a small proportion of our society involved in hard-core weight training, only a handful of people can be reached by catering to that segment of our population. Currently, about twenty percent of people living in the United States are involved in any kind of fitness program, and ten percent of those are floating in and out of fitness centers like waves pounding a shoreline. To expect a large percentage of these people to dedicate the time, effort, and lifestyle changes necessary to achieve the degree of physical development of a champion bodybuilder is anything but realistic.

On the other hand, a small number of weight training books come along that have a positive impact on the health and fitness industry and then go one step further. They draw more people into the slow growing numbers who are willing to invest the time, effort, and dedication it takes to make a difference in the quality of their lifestyle.

The Weight Training Workbook by Jim Bennett is such a book. It provides the tools, information, and motivation necessary to achieve realistic fitness goals.

This no-nonsense book leaves little to the imagination. It covers all the basics and has everything necessary to start a sound fitness program. The Weight Training Workbook takes the guess work out of weight training and shows you how to design and track your training programs. It leads you through the do's and don'ts that are so important when striving to achieve personal fitness goals. What isn't covered on resistance weight training in the The Weight Training Workbook probably isn't worth putting on paper.

Bill Pearl
Former Mr. America, Mr. USA, Mr. Universe

1
THE BASICS OF WEIGHT TRAINING

Weight Training Defined

Weight training is defined as progressive resistance exercise. This is a form of muscular exercise using resistance provided by barbells and dumbbells (free weights), or exercise machines to stimulate muscle growth and increase muscle strength and endurance. A weight training program consists of a series of different exercises grouped together by sets and repetitions. Repetitions (reps) are the number of complete and continuous executions of an exercise. Sets are the distinct groupings of repetitions performed.

The term weight training can be divided into four specific types of resistance exercise.

Bodybuilding — The objective of bodybuilding is to change the appearance of your body by exercising with progressively heavier weights. Depending on the objectives and training intensity, this type of activity will tone and firm or strengthen and increase the size of specific muscle groups.

Bodybuilding has gained increased popularity worldwide both as a means of improving general health and fitness and as a competitive sport for both men and women.

Competitive Lifting — In this division both men and women compete to lift the heaviest weight for one single repetition in a required exercise. The competitive lifts emphasize explosive power and speed and require great precision gained over years of intense training.

Sport Specific Training — Sport specific training is used by athletes to increase muscular strength and endurance. This form of overall conditioning will normally allow the athlete to improve in his or her specific sport.

Injury Rehabilitation — Weight training is recognized by sports medicine experts as a method of recovery from injury-weakened joints and muscles. Once the initial injury has healed, a prescribed weight training program can help strengthen damaged muscles and joints.

Now that you are familiar with the four divisions of weight training you can ask yourself, "Where do I fit in?" If you are not training for a competitive lift, trying to improve your performance in a specific sport, or recovering from an injury you are bodybuilding.

The Weight Training Environment

There are two options available when deciding where to train with weights. The first is your home. There is a wide selection of fitness equipment designed specifically for home use. If this is your decision, thoroughly research the advantages and disadvantages of each exercise equipment manufacturer. The equipment should allow you to perform several different exercises for each major muscle group.

Your second option is to workout in a gym or fitness center. Gyms and fitness centers can be found in high schools, colleges, YMCA's, community centers, corporations, hospitals, resorts, aircraft carriers, and law enforcement agencies, to name only a few. When shopping for a fitness center, always check for instructor certification. If a fitness center advertises it has trained, certified instructors, ask to look at each instructor's certification. If they try to skirt the issue, move on. A well managed fitness center will have certified staff ready to answer all your questions, especially if you are a new member with little or no knowledge of the training principles or exercises associated with weight training.

Since cost is a major factor when purchasing a fitness center membership, be sure to perform a complete and thorough inspection. Check the equipment for damage and regular maintenance, locker rooms and showers for cleanliness, safety features such as catch racks and collars for barbells, exercise rooms with adequate space, and sufficient ventilation and air conditioning. The final step in your inspection is to ask other persons using the fitness center their opinion of the advantages and disadvantages of a membership. When it passes your inspection and you feel confident about the staff and type of membership offered, then sign your check and prepare to begin weight training.

Workout Clothing

The weight training environment will dictate the type of clothing to be worn. There may be instances when guidelines must be followed concerning proper workout apparel. When deciding what to wear, keep in mind that it should be loose-fitting or made with spandex or elastic material to allow movement through a full range of motion.

A Weight Training Partner

The best way to maintain a strong commitment to achieving your long-term fitness goals is with a training partner. You are not likely to miss a workout if you are obligated to meet your training partner at the gym at a specific time. As you train together, you will develop a competitive edge which will drive each of you to workout with a greater degree of determination and intensity.

Beating your last best set or rep or your partners is a very satisfying and rewarding accomplishment. A training partner will help significantly if you have set a target completion date to achieve your fitness goals.

Establishing Fitness Goals

Knowledge and a strong commitment will help you to achieve your weight training goals and take advantage of the life-long health benefits associated with general fitness and competitive bodybuilding. In general, most gym and fitness center members are unfamiliar with weight training, and as a result, unrealistically expect to achieve fitness goals within a short period of time. Knowledge, combined with a strong commitment, and time are the only building blocks that will allow you to successfully achieve specific weight training goals.

The first question to ask when establishing your fitness goal is, "Specifically, what do I want to accomplish?" Don't just say you want to improve your health, but establish specific goals such as reducing your body measurements a pre-determined number of inches or increasing your bench press a specific number of pounds. The next step is to determine your beginning level of fitness. You can ask your personal physician or fitness center to conduct a fitness evaluation to establish a beginning reference point. With your fitness goals and starting point well established, you can now concentrate on achieving your first month goal.

It is important to record your short- and long-term fitness goals. If your long-term goal is to build muscle size and strength, then ask a certified fitness professional to help you write an action plan and set a realistic short-term goal to gain a predetermined amount of strength and size per month. Working toward achieving a monthly short-term goal will add to your motivation by providing a greater sense of accomplishment.

Weight training progress can be easily measured if you keep a record of your weight training goals, monthly changes in body measurements, and daily workouts. This will help you to evaluate your progress and keep you focused on achieving your long-term fitness goals. An equally strong motivator to help keep you focused on achieving a specific fitness goal is setting a target completion date. Several factors must be considered when determining a target completion date, such as beginning level of fitness, degree of proposed change, anticipated rate of progress, and outside influences (illness, holidays, school, work schedule, etc.). After you have carefully evaluated each variable, you will be able to set a realistic and attainable target completion date.

> **Important:** Before beginning any type of exercise program, it is important to consult your physician if you are 35 years of age or older, have not been involved in a regular exercise program, smoke, have signs of high blood pressure, or use a pacemaker. If your fitness goals are realistic and attainable your physician will give you the go-ahead that will increase your incentive to start your weight training without hesitation.

The Measurement Record

Weight training goals must be measured to determine if and when they have been reached. Establish a starting point from which progress will be measured by having your beginning measurements recorded on the first day of your weight training program – before you start your first exercise. Always have your measurements taken again at one-month intervals.

Next, determine the short-term measurement goals you want to achieve by the end of the first month. Under the column "1st Mo./Goal" enter your short-term goals. At the end of the first month have your measurements taken again and compare them with your goals. Set new goals for the next month and work toward achieving them. If you have determined a realistic target completion date you will begin to see a month-by-month progression toward achieving your fitness goals on or around the date you have set.

The term "RHR" represents your resting heart rate. To determine your resting heart rate take your pulse during a period of minimum stress. This can be accomplished by taking your pulse first thing in the morning before you get out of bed. Your resting heart rate, in comparison with your target heart rate (70%) for most bodybuilders (220 minus your age, then multiplied by 0.7), will give you an indication of your cardiovascular fitness. For example, if you are 35 years old, subtract 35 from 220 which equals 185. Then multiply 185 by 0.7. Your answer is a target heart rate of 130.

The term "% Fat" represents your percentage of body fat. This can be determined mathematically using your body measurements, mechanically using a caliper which pinches the skin, hydrostatically using water or electronically using a small electric current passing through your body. Each method is used to determine the ratio of body fat to body mass.

Progress Graphs

Once again, your weight training fitness goals must be measured or there is no way of knowing if or when they have been reached. A simple and easy way to ensure that you are progressing toward your fitness goal is by using a Progress

Graph. Use the following example to set up a Progress Graph to follow your monthly changes in body weight.

Body Weight — At each one-month interval have your body weight and measurements taken and record the results in the Measurement Record. For accuracy, always have your measurements taken each month by the same person.

First, write in the first month your weight was measured under the first vertical line. Make a dot representing your present body weight at the intersection of the highest horizontal line and move down the vertical line writing in 5 pound increments as shown below.

Second, realistically determine a completion month and move up that vertical line until you reach your goal weight. Draw a reference line between your present weight and goal weight. After one month have your body weight measured again and place a dot at the intersection of the month and body weight. Repeat this procedure each month to until you reach your body weight goal.

<u>Important:</u> Before beginning a Progress Graph, always ensure that your fitness goal is realistic and attainable.

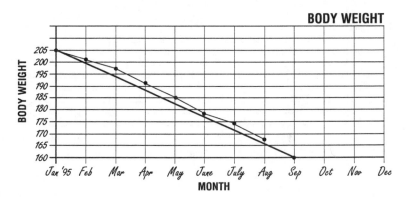

If your fitness goal is to increase your muscle size and strength use a Progress Graph to track your body measurements and lifting poundage. To establish the parameters of a muscle size and strength Progress Graph, perform a 3-rep max strength test for the bench press, shoulder press, leg press, bicep curl, lat pulldown, and triceps extension. Always ask for a spotter when performing a 3-rep max strength test.

Example: To set up the Bench Press Progress Graph, write in the first month your bench press was measured under the first vertical line and your starting bench press poundage on the first horizontal line. Make a dot at this intersection. Move up the vertical scale writing in 5 or 10 pound increments until you reach your bench press strength goal. Now realistically determine the number of months it will take to achieve your goal and write in the month under the appropriate vertical line. Place a dot at the intersection of the goal poundage and completion month and draw a reference line between the two dots, as shown below. Your Progress Graph is now ready for use.

The next month have your bench press strength measured and place a dot at the intersection of the appropriate

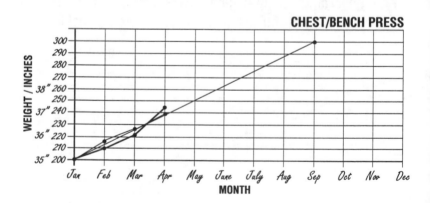

month and weight pressed. Repeat this procedure each month to until you reach your bench press strength goal.

If your bench press strength goal also includes increasing your chest measurement you can track your progress along with your strength goal by assigning an inch measure to left side of the graph. Using a different colored pencil, establish your starting point on the graph and each month before you begin to determine your bench press strength ask to have your chest measured.

The Daily
Weight Training Record

Realizing progress or re-establishing fitness goals is accomplished by maintaining an accurate record of each workout. Recording the exercises, sets, reps, weights, and workout comments during each workout will help you to look back over a period of time to determine the amount and rate of progress. This will further add to your determination to achieve your long-term fitness goals and weight training objectives.

Along the top of the training record are spaces for recording the date, time of day, and your body weight. The lines below "Exercise" is where you will record the names of the various exercises performed, followed by the number of repetitions executed and weight used for up to six sets. Along the bottom of the page is space to record notes regarding the circumstances affecting your workout, and daily calorie, protein, carbohydrate, and fat intake. It is to your benefit to record daily nutritional intake, mood, length and quality of the previous night's sleep, and any other factors that may affect the quality of your workout.

When you have exhausted the weight training records you can use The Weight Training Record as a means of maintaining an accurate record of daily workouts for up to one year.

The Eight Basic
Principles Of Weight Training

Weight training is individualized and can only be designed according to your particular anatomy, physiological condition and fitness goals. Since no two people have the same body type, height or weight, they stand little chance of attaining the same results if they train identically. So how do you determine which is the best weight training program for you? The answer lies in understanding and applying the eight basic principles of weight training and evaluating their effects.

1. Overload — This principle is defined as increasing the resistance to movement or frequency and duration of activity. To stimulate an increase in muscle size, strength, and endurance you must go beyond the regular activity level your muscles are accustomed to experiencing on a day-to-day basis. Without overloading your muscles, it will be impossible to achieve any significant gains. The four methods used to overload muscles are:

1. Increasing the resistance.
2. Increasing the number of repetitions.
3. Increasing the rate of work.
4. Increasing the amount of work in the same time period.

Each method is different and should be included in your training program with the percentages of each varying according to your fitness goals and weight training objectives. In general, increasing the resistance will promote increased muscle size and strength; increasing the number of repetitions performed will promote improved muscle endurance; increasing the rate of work will give you more power; and increasing the amount of work performed will provide greater gains in your overall strength and endurance. Too much of an in*r* result in overtraining.

2. Universality — This is defined as the all-around devel opment principle. You must develop muscle strength and endurance together with all the major muscles, joints and support structures. Universality will serve as a base for high intensity, specialized training and development which is essential for competitive bodybuilding and other sports.

3. Gradualness — The demands placed on your muscles must progress gradually in both volume and intensity. Physical ability and immediate level of fitness will determine your rate of increase. No matter how hard you try, you will not realize significant improvement in a short period of time. The only method known to achieve long-lasting results is to adhere to gradualness. This can not be over-emphasized. If you reach a plateau in your weight training, do not become alarmed. It may be an indication that you need to vary one or more of these eight weight training principles.

4. Progressiveness — This principle is closely related to gradualness and overload. When stimulating muscle to adapt to greater workloads, over a period of time there must be a progressive increase in the amount of weight used. This weight increase will be greater in the beginning phase of weight training and become less when muscles become more developed.

5. Repetition — Performing repetitions with light to moderate weight is the best way to learn how to properly perform an exercise and provoke physiological changes to take place in your body. Performing repetitions in a slow, rhythmical and deliberate manner will help you to develop the proper exercise technique. If you begin using heavy weights, you will not learn correct technique. When your technique is faulty, you will not be working the muscle properly. This can lead to possible injury.

6. Consistency — To realize any change in muscle size, strength and body measurements you must commit to a regular weight training schedule. The minimum being two days a week. Your body will respond only when exercises are performed on a regular basis. This is where you come face-to-face with your commitment to achieve specific health and fitness goals. Achieving maximum results will require a strong commitment to your workouts and training objectives.

7. Individualism — Your age, sex, body type, metabolism, and predisposition for muscle growth will limit you from achieving the same results as another person following the same weight training routine. Therefore, it is unrealistic to think that you can achieve the identical results as that of any other person. You can implement the same training techniques, but the results you experience will be specific to your own individuality.

Individualism should also be considered when choosing food supplements to support your weight training. In general, it's a matter of trial and error to find the proper food supplements that will enhance your weight training and provide maximum results.

One characteristic if individualism is the limited ability to recover, or the capacity of your metabolism to compensate for the effects of exercise. Therefore, to achieve an increase in muscle strength and size it is important to carefully consider individuality and appropriately regulate the training stimulus in terms of volume and frequency.

8. Awareness — Knowledge is the key to achieving specific fitness goals. With knowledge as your foundation, you will maintain a long-term focus on your commitment, and pursue your fitness goals with a greater enthusiasm.

In general, most people working out in gyms and fitness centers lack the basic knowledge and understanding needed to achieve the fitness goals they have set out to accomplish. As a result, they begin their first day of weight training by imitating the actions and thinking of the people working out around them. Subsequently, their knowledge is based on the assumption that the people they are imitating have an understanding of the basic principles of weight training. This is often referred to as "Monkey See – Monkey Do."

Without knowledge, even the finest fitness equipment will yield poor results.

Gaining Weight
And Building Muscle

Gaining weight and building muscle is very simple. First, begin a progressive resistance exercise program; and second, redesign your diet to support the activity specific to your long-term fitness goals. These are the only two building blocks that will allow you to achieve your desired results. Using progressively heavier weights and varying the training intensity will promote increased muscle size and strength as your body begins to adapt to the new demands. You must also modify your diet and eating schedule to accommodate up to six smaller meals throughout the day. Each meal should include foods which contain a greater amount of protein and carbohydrate calories. This will fuel muscle recovery and growth.

Your muscles are made of protein. Therefore, you need more than just protein to achieve gains in strength and size. To satisfy your basic metabolic requirements you must eat foods to replace the carbohydrates, fat, and protein metabolized each day. This is accomplished by proportionately increasing your non-protein calories and protein consumption. This will provide the additional protein your body will require for muscle recovery and growth.

When daily protein and carbohydrate consumption is less than what is required to adequately fuel your weight training, your progress will slow down or virtually stop. If this is the case, your body will begin using muscle (protein) for energy. When training to increase muscle strength and size, and an increased amount of protein and carbohydrate calories are available in your diet, you will begin to make greater achievements toward your fitness goals.

Muscle Strength And Endurance

To achieve the full benefits from weight training, it is necessary to develop and maintain a well-rounded training program that exercises all the major muscle groups. Muscle strength and endurance can only be developed by the overload principle. This is accomplished by increasing the amount of weight used or increasing the frequency and duration of sets and reps performed.

Muscular strength is best developed by using heavier weights and performing 6-8 repetitions. Muscle endurance is developed by using lighter weight and performing 10-25 repetitions. To some extent, muscular strength and endurance are developed using each method, but each favors a more specific development. The intensity of your weight training can be changed by varying the amount of weight used, speed and number of repetitions performed, number of sets, and length of the rest interval between sets. To gain improvement in both muscular strength and endurance, most experts recommend 8-12 repetitions per set.

Any degree of overload will result in strength development, but performing repetitions at or near 80-90 percent of your one rep maximum will stimulate a substantial increase in muscle strength and size. Your expected gains are limited to your initial level of strength and predisposition for improvement.

To achieve the greatest gains, keep your routine rhythmical, performed at a moderate to slow speed, and for maximum benefit always perform the exercise through its full range of motion. The combination and interaction of frequency, intensity, and duration of exercise is the most effective method for achieving an increase in muscle size, strength and endurance.

"No Pain–No Gain"

The expression "No Pain–No Gain" was prevalent in the fifties as athletes were driven by their coaches to work at or above their maximum performance level. They were often told that pain, either physical or psychological, was an indication of work output. This may be the motive of the well developed bodybuilder or powerlifter, but it is not the case for the general fitness bodybuilder. Significant gains are attainable without subjecting yourself to this type of pain.

Weight training is the ideal activity to stimulate the anaerobic metabolic process. The discomfort experienced in your muscles is a result of the by-products of anaerobic metabolism. The chief fuels are glucose and glycogen. As a result of the breakdown of these fuels, "fatigue acids" (lactic and pyruvic) are produced. It is only when these acids reach a critical level that they irritate nerve endings close to the muscle fibers. This irritation is what causes muscle discomfort. It is through this biochemical process that muscle growth is stimulated.

It is important to become aware of and know the difference between discomfort and pain. Not all pain experienced is a positive sign of maximum muscle stimulation. Duration of pain is one of the primary ways of distinguishing between the two. The discomfort experienced with anaerobic metabolism is normally short in duration.

Your body will begin to produce natural chemicals known as "buffers" to reduce the acidity. Thus, the discomfort experienced with weight training will normally subside within one to three days. Pain that does not subside after a few days is usually an indication of a possible muscle pull, strain, sprain, or tendon/ligament damage. In most cases, this type of pain will become more acute and intense. If this is the case, it is recommended that you stop training and consult your physician. Treatments for such pain will include rest, cold compress and elevation of the injured body part.

When pain is experienced during a set and does not rapidly diminish during the rest interval, you may have sustained an injury. This type of pain may need to be examined by a physician before proceeding.

If it takes longer than it should for your muscles to recover following a workout, this might be due in part to your circulatory system. The circulatory system delivers and distributes nutrients required for muscle growth and removes waste products produced by weight training. Without a healthy circulatory system, your body will have difficulty recovering before the next workout.

Weight Training Safety

The introduction of weight training safety is often a neglected topic in gyms and fitness centers. When one individual fails to follow proper safety procedures, he or she, along with other people nearby, become candidates for injury. For this reason, it is important to become familiar with and incorporate the following safety rules into your weight training:

■ **Before use, inspect equipment for wear and tear.** Before beginning an exercise, walk around the equipment to look for worn or loose fittings, frayed cables, and dry, unlubricated guide rods.

■ **Use a spotter when performing demanding exercises.** Always use a spotter when using heavy weights. If you are not sure of your ability, ask another person to spot you.

■ **Weight training alone.** When weight training at home or at a gym with few people around, make another person aware of your activities and ask them to check on you periodically.

■ **Barbell catch racks.** A barbell catch rack is used to hold the barbell before performing exercises such as the bench press or squat. When used properly, a catch rack will allow you to safely perform the exercise and prevent an errant barbell from causing injury to yourself and others.

■ **Barbell collars.** Barbell collars are metal clamps placed on the ends of a barbell to prevent the weight plates from sliding off when performing an exercise. If your fitness center or gym does not have collars available for your use, insist that they get some.

■ **Wear a weight lifting belt.** Weight lifting belts come in a wide variety of widths, thicknesses, and material. Leather belts are often times too stiff and can cause cuts and bruises. Fabric weight belts are more flexible and comfortable because of their ability to conform to the contours of your body. The most important factor to consider when purchasing a weight lifting belt is the width of the front of the belt. The belt works by pressurizing the internal abdominal cavity, so the width of the belt in the rear is of little value.

The intra-abdominal pressure, or IAP, is created by contracting the abdominal and spinal muscles causing the spine to be held more rigid and its natural forward curvature straightened to eliminate most uncontrolled twisting and compression stress. The higher the IAP, the greater the lifting load the spine can support without injury.

When used properly, a belt will protect your abdominals and back from possible injury when performing heavy movements, such as the squat and deadlift. Wearing a weight lifting belt comfortably snug (not tight) during low intensity activities will provide relief from low back aches and help you to exercise longer.

Important: Wearing a tightly cinched weight lifting belt when resting or performing less than demanding exercises can significantly raise your blood pressure.

Lifts which heavily load the spine, such as squats, deadlifts, calf raises, and bent-over rows, should be performed wearing a weight lifting belt. Wearing a belt when performing exercises such as the behind-the-neck press, military press, and standing arm curl will help you maintain a more stable trunk posture.

There are exercises in which wearing a belt will provide little benefit, such as the bench press. During the bench press you will normally perform the Valsalva maneuver during the exercise which consists of taking a deep breath seconds before lifting a very heavy weight.

■ **Never hold your breath.** Holding your breath beyond what is required for the initial movement will limit the flow of oxygen to your brain and may cause dizziness. If held too long, it could cause you to black out.

It makes no difference how you breathe as long as you breathe during the exercise. When you are not sure, the best thing to do is to breathe normally. This will prevent you from blacking out or experiencing a feeling of dizziness.The most often used breathing pattern is inhaling during least resistance and exhaling during maximum resistance.

■ **Return equipment when finished.** When you finish performing an exercise always return weight plates, dumbbells, barbells, and miscellaneous equipment to their appropriate location. Leaving them on the floor or propped up against a wall will only be setting yourself or another person up for possible injury. When the equipment is returned to its proper place, you will not have to search the gym or fitness center for that one missing item. This is just common courtesy.

■ **Train with a certified instructor.** If your fitness center or gym advertises that they have trained, certified instructors on staff, by all means make good use of them. New members most often weight train without supervision and imitate other people performing unfamiliar exercises. They then attempt to perform the same exercise themselves. This is referred to as "Monkey See – Monkey Do." The new gym member could sustain possible injury because they may not understand the exercise and specific precautions. A certified fitness instructor can prevent the development of poor form and bad habits.

■ **Always warm-up before and cool-down after weight training.** Beginning your weight training without a proper warm-up can subject you to possible injury. A proper warm-up will increase your pulse rate, overall body temperature, blood and oxygen flow to specific muscles, and mentally prepare you for your weight training session. If you are limited by time, a few laps around the running track or a few minutes on a stationary bike or stepping machine is better than performing no warm-up at all.

The two types of warm-up programs are general and specific. The general warm-up includes large muscle activities such as aerobics, jogging, skipping rope, stationary cycling and stretching, and should last 10-15 minutes. The specific warm-up will prepare the muscle group to be exercised by performing 1-2 light, but progressively heavier sets prior to weight training with heavy weights.

The cool-down should immediately follow your weight training and should last 5-15 minutes. This will allow your body to recover from your weight training session and begin to cool down. The cool-down should include the same activities as the general warm-up, but performed at a more casual pace, like easy power walking, jogging, stepping, and stationary cycling.

Sets, Reps
And Muscle Groups

The number of repetitions performed during each set will depend upon the muscle group being worked. The upper body muscle groups (chest, back, shoulders, upper arms) should be kept within the range of 8-12 reps per set. The legs within the range of 10-14 reps per set, and abdominal exercises between 25-100 reps per set. The calves and forearms respond best to 15-25 reps per set.

The number of repetitions performed will vary between muscle groups for the following two reasons: First, some muscles have a greater content of endurance-promoting fibers (slow-twitch muscle fibers), while others have a greater content of strength-promoting fibers (fast-twitch muscle fibers). Second, muscles that are used on a regular basis during the day are composed of muscle fibers that have been toughened to exercise and require additional stimulation with increased reps and weight.

Performing 4-6 reps with a moderately heavy weight will develop greater strength and muscle mass. Performing 8-12 reps with a lighter weight will produce greater endurance.

Varying Your Weight Training Program

Your body and its central nervous system are very adaptable to the intensity of the demands regularly experienced. If you continue to perform the same exercises using the same number of sets, reps, and weight – over a period of time your body will eventually adapt and begin to respond at an increasingly slower rate.

To consistently progress in achieving your fitness goals and training objectives, you must change the intensity of your workouts on a regular basis. This can be accomplished by varying one or more of the eight weight training principles.

Length of Rest Interval Between Sets

The rest interval between sets will depend upon your present level of fitness and exercise intensity. During an average weight training session you should rest up to one minute between sets. During an intense, advanced training session you may need to rest up to three minutes between sets. This will give your body time to recover from the previous set and prepare for the next one.

The rest interval will be shorter when working smaller muscle groups such as biceps and triceps, and longer when working larger muscle groups such as legs and back. If you begin to feel light-headed after a set, take an extended rest interval to regain your composure. Then try reducing the number of reps or amount of weight used in the next set.

Exercising
With Proper Form

The manner in which you perform an exercise is important if you are to striving to achieve maximum results from your weight training. Performing an exercise with proper form places the greatest load on the muscle group being worked. Sacrificing form for additional weight always yields poor results. Bringing other body parts into the movement, such as jerking, or swinging a weight or body part to get moving is called cheating and will yield poor results.

When performing an exercise, it is important to maintain the recommended body position and move the body joint/muscle through its full range of motion. The muscle being worked should be allowed to move from full extension to full contraction and back to full extension during each repetition. Movements shorter than this will not allow the muscle to work up to its full capacity.

A Beginning
Weight Training Program

It has been determined through testing and research that weight training only once a week offers only a marginal benefit. If you are committed to reducing weight and inches, gaining weight and building muscle mass, or establishing and maintaining a high level of physical fitness, you need to workout a minimum of 2-3 days each week. On alternate days perform cardiovascular exercise such as fast walking, stepping, stationary biking or jogging.

During the first month, after a 10-15 minute warm-up each weight training session should last no longer than one hour. One month of consistent weight training with light to progressively moderate weight will cause your body to become gradually accustomed to the activity. From that point on, you will begin to gain greater confidence during each workout and consider incorporating one or more high-intensity strength training techniques into your weight training.

The following is a suggested routine to begin your weight training program:

BEGINNING ROUTINE

Exercise	Sets	Reps
1. Five to ten minutes of warm-up exercises.	–	–
2. Crunches (abdominals)	2	25-40
3. Incline Bench Press (chest)	2-3	8-12
4. Seated Dumbbell Press (shoulders)	2-3	8-12
5. Bicep Curl (biceps)	2-3	8-10
6. Tricep Extension (triceps)	2	8-10
7. Lat Machine Pulldown (back)	2	8-12
8. Leg Extension (legs-quadriceps)	2-3	8-12
9. Leg Curl (legs-hamstrings)	3	8-12
10. Five to ten minutes of cool-down exercises.	–	–

You will have to rely on your own intuition and level of fitness to determine the appropriate amount of weight to use. When beginning your weight training program it is important to use less weight to familiarize yourself with the exercise. Once you have learned the exercise and can perform it correctly, gradually add weight. If a set calls for 8-12 reps and you can perform 15 comfortably, the weight is too light. Conversely, if you can not perform more than 6-8 reps, the weight is too heavy. Using this method will ensure correct intensity. Always move through your workout at a good pace.

Beginning weight training intensity is dependent upon your present level of fitness. Whenever you subject your muscles to a workload greater than they are accustomed to it will provoke muscle soreness and discomfort. To prevent severe muscle discomfort, gradually introduce your muscles to new exercises by starting with light weight. Any major or minor discomfort can be avoided when you follow a gradual weight training program during the first month.

Your initial training will consist of performing 1-3 light sets of each exercise during the first month. From there, you will gradually add more sets and weight until you experience little or no soreness. Once you have made it past the first month you can begin to increase the intensity of your workouts. This is accomplished by performing each set to muscle failure. When the weight has been well chosen, you should barely be able to complete your intended number of repetitions for each set.

Split Routines

During the first month of weight training you will workout a minimum of two non-consecutive days a week. This will give your muscles 48 hours between workouts to recover. A popular method to increase weight training intensity is to split your routine to work two or more major muscle groups on a different day. This is known as a split routine. In the basic sp' tine you will work three major muscle groups on Mond Thursday, and remaining muscle groups on Tuesday and Friday.

The following is an example of a four-day split routine. Abs and calves are worked on alternate days.

4-Day Routine

Monday - Thursday	Tuesday - Friday
Abs	Abs
Chest	Legs
Triceps	Biceps/Forearms
Shoulders	Back
Calves	Calves

To intensify your weight training even further, you can choose either a five- or six-day split routine. The five-day split routine divides your weight training so you are exercising the same muscle groups on alternate days. The following is an example of a five-day split routine. Every other Monday routine is alternated with Tuesday.

5-Day Routine

Monday - Wednesday - Friday	Tuesday - Thursday
Abs	Abs
Legs	Chest
Biceps/Forearms	Triceps
Back	Shoulders
Calves	Calves

The six-day split routine is the most intense workout program you can follow. This is normally the training schedule followed by men and women who are involved in advanced competitive bodybuilding. The following is an example of a six-day split routine.

6-Day Routine

Mon - Thurs	Tues - Fri	Wed - Sat
Abs	Abs	Abs
Chest	Triceps	Legs
Shoulders	Biceps	Back
Calves	Forearms	Calves

High-Intensity Strength Training

Several high-intensity strength training techniques can be used to produce a greater increase in muscle strength and size. The purpose of high-intensity training is to make your muscles work harder in a shorter period of time, rather than a longer period of time. This appears to be the best stimulus for increasing muscle strength and size.

Because of effects of high-intensity strength training on muscle tissue, the recovery process requires a longer period of time. Therefore, your weight training schedule should be carefully planned to provide one high-intensity workout per muscle group per week. This will provide the stimulus for optimum muscle development.

After performing a 10-15 minute general warm-up in preparation for your high-intensity training, the specific muscle group to be worked is then warmed up by performing several sets with a light weight. From here on, the remaining sets will be taken to the point of failure. This is when you can no longer complete a rep without additional help. There are two methods used to bring your muscles to the point of failure; forced reps, and strip sets. Other techniques such as compound sets, trisets, negative reps, and forced negatives will also increase the intensity of your weight training.

■ **Forced Reps** — Forced reps are performed with a training partner or spotter. After your muscle is taken to the point of failure, your training partner applies enough pressure to help you complete the rep. An example would be the bench press. Your training partner stands at the head of the bench and lightly pulls up on the bar with enough pressure to keep it moving. Each additional rep would require your training partner to apply more pressure.

■ **Strip Sets** — This is a method by which weight is progressively removed from an exercise machine or barbell during the execution of an exercise. Using the bench press as an example, place two spotters at opposite ends of the bar to remove a predetermined amount of weight each time you reach the point of failure. The bar should be loaded with a variety of weight plates so you can perform 4-6 repetitions with strict form. After reaching the point of failure, have each spotter remove a predetermined amount of weight from the bar. Perform another set until you reach the point of failure, and again, remove more weight. If you are still going strong, repeat the process again to the point of total muscle fatigue. When finished, you will experience a "pumped" sensation you have never felt before.

■ **Slow Sets** — Slow sets are performed by deliberately slowing down the pace of the exercise movement. Slower movements use less momentum and require a greater muscle force throughout the entire range of motion. Using the barbell bench press as an example – the bar is raised using a slow count to four and lowered using a slow count to six. This method can provide a greater increase in muscle strength and mass.

■ **Super Sets** — Super sets increase the intensity of your weight training by performing two or more exercises back-to-back with little to no rest between sets. To achieve maximum results, a rotary exercise for a specific muscle group is followed immediately by a linear exercise that works the same muscle group. An example would be dumbbell flyes followed by a set of the barbell bench press, or side lateral raises followed by a set of an overhead press.

■ **Negative Only Reps** — Negative reps are performed by lowering the weight at a much slower pace than it was raised. For example, if you want to perform five reps of a wide grip chin-up exercise, but are unable to perform a single rep, negative-only exercise would be an effective training technique. Because of the possibility of losing control when performing negative only reps, a training partner or spotter is recommended.

■ **Forced Negatives** — Forced negatives are performed with exercise machines and free weights. After the weight is raised, you will resist additional negative pressure being applied by your training partner or spotter. When performing pure negatives, you will be able to use a weight 30-50% heavier. Your training partner will provide the necessary assistance to raise the weight to the starting position.

Post-Workout Recovery

Your muscles grow in size and strength when you *are not* weight training. In other words, the muscle recovery and growth process is at work not only when you are not weight training, but when you are completely at rest. If you have provided your metabolism with an adequate supply of protein and carbohydrates, anabolism will reach its peak when you are experiencing high-quality sleep. Once asleep, the growth hormone testosterone continues to increase beginning late afternoon and reaches its peak in the early morning. The growth hormone cortisol, an anti-inflammatory catabolic hormone follows an opposite pattern.

The recovery process will take from 48-72 hours depending on the intensity of your weight training. This process itself will require you to rest periodically during the day and achieve high-quality sleep in the evening. Periodic resting consists of taking a 15 to 30 minute rest period, evenly spaced during the day. This may become a necessity when the intensity of your weight training has increased or when you find yourself becoming over-stressed.

A rest period involves lying down or reclining on a soft surface and letting go both physically and mentally. This will normally refresh and recharge your energy level. Sleep requirements vary considerably between individuals. The norm for most people is eight hours of sleep a night. Some individuals function at 100% with only four or five hours per night and others require ten to twelve hours before they consider beginning their day. Let your body dictate how much sleep you need. This will allow you to rise alert, energetic, and ready to begin your day.

Overtraining

There are two types of overtraining, general and local. General overtraining affects the whole body producing stagnation and decreased physical performance. When local overtraining occurs, only one specific body part or muscle group is affected. Local overtraining can be experienced by most persons involved in weight training and is recognized by soreness and stiffness after performing a particular exercise.

When overtraining is not acknowledged and allowed to become serious, it can take weeks or even months for your body to recover. Overtraining must not be confused with exhaustion. Exhaustion is a reaction to the short-term imbalance between stress and how your body is adapting to it. Overtraining is the result of a prolonged imbalance with many obvious characteristics. It is important to understand and recognize the warning signs of overtraining and take the necessary steps to alleviate the problem before it gets worse.

The following characteristics can be used to identify an "overtrained" condition:

- You experience a noticeable decrease in your strength or performance level.

- Insomnia. You have a difficult time falling asleep.

- You experience a slow, general increase in muscle soreness and stiffness after a workout.

- Fatigue. You sleep longer than normal and still feel tired.

- Consistently elevated blood pressure.

- Elevated resting heart rate (10 bpm higher than normal for several days in a row). Check your resting heart rate in the morning before getting out of bed. If your resting heart rate is higher than normal, your metabolism has not yet recovered from the previous workout. It normally takes 90 minutes to 2 hours for your pulse to return to normal, even after a short workout.

- The recovery time between sets and workouts is longer than normal.

- Loss of appetite. This could be one of the reasons for a decrease in body weight.

- Your coordination becomes impaired. It has become difficult to perform exercises at the same pace and with the same coordination you experienced during previous workouts.

- Depression. You become psychologically and emotionally drained. This includes increased nervousness, irritability, inability to relax and poor motivation.

Overtraining is caused by training at an intensity that does not allow your metabolism to properly recover before the next workout. Your body has a limited capacity to adapt in a short period of time, and when it is over-stressed you will begin to experience one or more of the symptoms of overtraining.

Fluid Replacement

The body is made up of about 65% water. It is important to overcome fluid loss that inevitably accompanies vigorous, high-intensity exercise by consuming fluids. The importance of hydration can not be overstated: As little as a 1% decrease in body weight due to dehydration can significantly decrease performance. For example, the performance of a 200-pound athlete would be affected by a two-pound loss of body weight. Plain water may be an acceptable fluid replacement beverage. However, water can remove the biological urge to drink, which is why it is highly recommended to drink sports beverages.

Make sure the sports drink you choose contains up to 6 to 7 percent carbohydrate in the form of glucose, sucrose or maltodextrin; is not carbonated, contains electrolytes, tastes good during exercise, does not cause gastrointestinal distress when consumed in large volumes; and is rapidly absorbed.

Understanding Your Basal Metabolic Rate (BMR)

To properly fuel your weight training program, it is important to be aware of the number of calories your body requires each day. Approximately 60-70 percent of your body's energy is used to support the continuous metabolic work of your body's cells. This is referred to as your basal metabolic rate or BMR. The continual work and maintenance performed by your body includes the beating of your heart, respiration, and the maintenance of your body temperature. Your body requires that its energy needs be met before any calories can be used for food digestion or physical activity.

The following factors affect your basal metabolic rate:

Age. Your basal metabolic rate changes with age. During childhood and adolescence, your BMR is higher due to the increased activity of cells undergoing division. Your BMR peaks at age 20 and then decreases by 2 percent per decade throughout your life. This is the same for both men and women.

Height. Taller people have a greater amount of body surface and as a result require a faster BMR.

Gender. Men have a greater percentage of lean tissue than women and as a result have a 10-15 percent faster metabolic rate. Lean tissue uses more calories than fat tissue. Therefore, an increase in muscle mass elevates the BMR. This is the same for both men and women.

Fasting and Dieting. Your BMR can drop as much as 20 percent when fasting or dieting. This metabolic reduction is due primarily to your body's attempt to conserve energy. Based on a food shortage, it is a protective mechanism to conserve fat stores.

Environmental Temperature. Exposure to both hot and cold temperatures will raise your body's BMR. People living in warmer climates will experience a 5-20 percent higher metabolism than those living in more temperate climates. Weight training in a hot, unventilated fitness center or outside in the heat will also raise your BMR.

Exercise. Research has not substantiated the effect of exercise on your basal metabolic rate. Since one method of increasing your basal metabolic rate is to increase your lean body mass, becoming involved in some form of regular exercise will help you achieve a higher BMR.

Determining Your BMR

Use the following formula to determine your BMR:

Adult Males. Multiply your body weight by 10; add double your body weight to this value. For example, for a 175 lb male: 1,750 + (2 x 175) = 2,100 cal/day BMR

Adult Females. Multiply your body weight by 10; add your body weight to this value. For example, for a 120 lb female: 1,200 + 120 = 1,320 cal/day BMR

Fueling Your Weight Training Program

[1]The National Research Council has established Recommended Dietary Allowances (RDA) for people involved in a moderate to active level of activity.

The following represents the number of calories required each day by activity level:

Level of Activity	Men	Women
Sedentary	16 cal./lb	14 cal./lb

Activities that involve sitting most the day, such as desk work and studying.

Light	17 cal./lb	16 cal./lb

Activities that involve standing or being on your feet most of the day.

Moderate	21 cal./lb	18 cal./lb

General fitness bodybuilding, housework, walking 4 mph.

Active	26 cal./lb	22 cal./lb

High Intensity bodybuilding, dancing, and manual labor such as farm or construction work.

Use the following example to determine your daily calorie requirements at your present weight based on your level of activity:

Example: A moderately active man involved in general fitness weight training weighs 150 pounds. To determine his maximum daily calorie requirements, he multiplies his body weight by 21, which equals 3,150. This figure represents the total number of calories his metabolism requires <u>each day</u> to maintain itself and adequately fuel his weight training activity.

Your ideal weight is determined by your sex, height and frame size. Use the following table to determine your average ideal weight. (Keep in mind, this table is unreliable for determining a <u>normal</u> body weight based on age and gender.) When you have determined your ideal body weight, use the same formula, (i.e. ideal body weight of 160 pounds, multiplied by 21, equals 3,360 calories per day). In our example, to reach an ideal body weight of 160 lbs., would require 3,360 calories each day or <u>210 additional</u> calories beyond what is required to remain at a present body weight of 150. To reach an ideal weight of 140, he would have to consume <u>210 fewer</u> calories than what is required to remain at his present body weight.

MEN				WOMEN			
Height Ft In	Small Frame	Medium Frame	Large Frame	Height Ft In	Small Frame	Medium Frame	Large Frame
5 2	128-134	131-141	138-150	4 10	102-111	109-121	118-131
5 3	130-136	133-143	140-153	4 1	1103-113	111-123	120-134
5 4	132-138	135-145	142-156	5 0	104-115	113-126	122-137
5 5	134-140	137-148	144-160	5 1	106-118	115-129	125-140
5 6	136-142	139-151	146-164	5 2	108-121	118-132	128-143
5 7	138-145	142-154	149-168	5 3	111-124	121-135	131-147
5 8	140-148	145-157	152-172	5 4	114-127	124-138	134-151
5 9	142-151	148-160	155-176	5 5	117-130	127-141	137-155
5 10	144-154	151-163	158-180	5 6	120-133	130-144	140-159
5 11	146-157	154-166	161-184	5 7	123-136	133-147	143-163
6 0	149-160	157-170	164-188	5 8	126-139	136-150	146-167
6 1	152-164	160-174	168-192	5 9	129-142	139-153	149-170
6 2	155-168	164-178	172-197	5 10	132-145	142-156	152-173
6 3	158-172	167-182	176-202	5 11	135-148	145-159	155-176
6 4	162-176	171-187	181-207	6 0	135-148	145-159	155-176

Build study, Society of Actuaries and Association of Life Insurance Medical Directors of America.

Basic Nutritional Information

1. One calorie contains the energy required to raise the temperature of one Kilogram of water one degree Centigrade.

2. One pound of body fat contains approximately 3,500 calories.

3. Fat provides the body with energy required between meals and during prolonged exercise.

4. The three basic food sources required by the body are carbohydrate, protein and fat. Carbohydrates and fat are used by the body for energy. Protein is used for building tissue and body maintenance.

5. Fat contains 9 calories per gram; protein contains 4 calories per gram; and carbohydrates contain 4 calories per gram.

6. When you consume more calories than your body requires, the extra calories will be stored as fat for future use.

7. Your daily diet must be nutritious, balanced and include an adequate amount of the basic nutrients: protein, carbohydrates, fat, vitamins, minerals, and water.

Protein Intake

Protein is used to build, repair, and maintain muscle, ligaments and tendons. It is not a primary energy source. When involved in weight training, muscle tissue is broken down and a process called anabolism rebuilds the muscle. Protein is what drives the anabolism process. When the amount of protein in your diet increases, your body will build new muscle tissue. If protein intake is insufficient, protein (muscle) will be broken down and used for energy.

To determine the amount of protein in your present diet conduct a nutritional inventory of your food intake during the past 24 hours and record the results in the following table:

Meal	Total Calories	Protein Grams	Carbohydrate Grams	Fat Grams
Breakfast				
Lunch				
Dinner				
Snacks				
Total				

[2]The recommended amount of daily protein consumption for persons involved in weight training is 1.76 grams per kilogram of body weight. Unfortunately, the body has a limit to the amount of protein it can use for building muscle. Excess protein may be converted to fat. At a weight of 160 pounds (73kg), you would require a minimum of 128 grams of protein each day. No net gains or losses are realized with a protein consumption of 1.41 grams per kilogram of body weight.

Therefore, any increase in dietary protein consumption above 1.41 g/kgbw will allow the body to form more proteins, a process stimulated by weight training. Use the chart on the next page to determine your specific protein needs.

This doesn't mean the more protein you eat above and beyond 1.76 g/kgbw, the greater gains you will achieve in muscle strength and size. [2]A protein intake of 2.4 g/kgbw will not provide any additional benefits.

Typical sources of protein are egg whites, skinless chicken (white meat), skinless turkey (white meat), and fish. Don't limit your meals to breakfast, lunch, and dinner alone. Your metabolism can only assimilate up to 30 grams of protein at each meal. The rest is stored for energy.

Suggested Daily Protein Consumption

Body Weight	KG/Body Weight	Protein	Body Weight	KG/Body Weight	Protein
100	45	80 gm	200	91	160 gm
110	50	88 gm	205	93	164 gm
115	52	92 gm	210	95	168 gm
120	54	96 gm	215	98	172 gm
125	57	100 gm	220	100	176 gm
130	59	104 gm	225	102	180 gm
135	61	108 gm	230	104	184 gm
140	64	112 gm	235	107	188 gm
145	66	116 gm	240	109	192 gm
150	68	120 gm	245	111	196 gm
155	70	124 gm	250	113	200 gm
160	73	128 gm	255	116	204 gm
165	75	132 gm	260	118	208 gm
170	77	136 gm	265	120	212 gm
175	79	140 gm	270	122	216 gm
180	82	144 gm	275	125	220 gm
185	84	148 gm	280	127	224 gm
190	86	152 gm	285	129	228 gm
195	88	156 gm	290	132	232 gm

Grams are rounded up to the nearest whole number.

Try to structure your schedule to eat 5-6 small meals throughout the day. In addition to the typical sources of protein there are many excellent high protein foods and supplements available to help increase your protein intake without increasing fat intake.

Carbohydrate Intake

Carbohydrates are the least abundant nutrient stored in the body and the main source of fuel for energy. Nutritionists recommend that your diet contain 60 to 65 percent carbohydrates when involved in intense physical activity. This recommendation equals a daily carbohydrate intake of about 3 to 4 grams per pound of body weight.

During digestion, complex carbohydrates are broken down into glucose. Glucose travels through the circulatory system as the main source of energy for refueling liver and muscle glycogen burned during exercise. Simple sugars are divided into two categories. Monosaccharides such as the glucose and fructose in fruit, and disaccharides such as lactose, or milk sugar which is made up of glucose and galactose. In some instances, simple sugars can cause a relatively sharp increase in blood sugar which can cause increased insulin release resulting in increased fat storage.

Starchy carbohydrates are made up of polysaccharides and provide a slower, more steady release of glucose into the bloodstream. Glucose from starchy carbohydrates causes minimum insulin secretion and provides greater sustained energy levels. A popular source of starchy carbohydrates is oatmeal, grits, potatoes, sweet potatoes, brown rice, yams, lima beans, kidney beans, peas, lentils, and other legumes. Fibrous plants and salad vegetables such as asparagus, broccoli, cauliflower, carrots, celery, green beans, and zucchini slow the release of carbohydrates into the bloodstream even more.

Fat Intake

To use fat as an effective source of energy, sufficient carbohydrate must be present in your diet. Understanding the various types of fat will help you in achieving the reduction in body fat required to meet your specific fitness goals.

Essential fatty acids (EFAs) are important in numerous biological functions, including prostaglandins, which are necessary to help regulate almost every system in your body. EFAs are essential to properly fuel your body for weight training. They are used in several muscle building processes such as increasing glutamine levels, releasing growth hormone, and keeping connective tissue and cell membranes strong and healthy.

If you are maintaining a low-fat diet, a supplement may be necessary to provide an adequate supply of EFAs. A popular source of EFAs is sunflower, safflower, linseed, or flaxseed oil.

Foods containing body fat such as beef are referred to as long-chain triglycerides (LCTs). LCTs must first be broken down in the intestines before they can be digested. Enzymes reduce the fat into fatty acids which travel across the membrane of the intestines where they are converted back into fat. At this point, they are transported by the lymphatic system to the neck and released into the circulatory system. This is the type of fat you want to avoid.

The American Heart Association advises that the percentage of fat calories in the American diet should be 30% or less. To reduce body fat, people involved in weight training should limit their fat calorie intake to 20–25 percent.

Use the following formula to calculate the percentage of fat calories in a food item:

1. Check the nutritional information for total calories and grams of fat per serving.

2. Multiply the number of fat grams by 9. This will give you the number of calories from fat.

3. Divide the number of calories from fat by the number of calories in a serving. The answer will be less than 1.

4. Multiply this number by 100 to get the percentage of calories from fat. If a serving of swiss cheese has 110 calories and 8 grams of fat, multiply 8 by 9 to get 72. Then divide 72 by 110 to get .65 and multiply by 100. The cheese you are eating yields 65% of its calories from fat.

[1]National Academy of Sciences, *Recommended Dietary Allowances*. 1980, 9th edition.

[2]Tarnopolsky M.A., Atkinson S.A., MacDougal J.D. et al. Evaluation of protein requirements of trained strength athletes. *Journal of Applied Physiology*. 1992;73:1986-95.

Reducing Your Percentage of Body Fat

Reducing your percentage of body fat is very simple – become involved in a regular low-intensity cardiovascular exercise program and reduce the amount of fat calories you consume by becoming knowledgeable of the nutritional content of the foods you frequently eat. These are the only two building blocks that can produce a lean, healthy, functional, and vibrant body. Fad diets, diet pills, or fasting will not provide the lasting results you can achieve from understanding your eating habits and becoming involved in a regular cardiovascular exercise program.

Weight training (anaerobic) alone will not improve your cardiovascular (aerobic) endurance. Rather weight training, combined with cardiovascular training such as running, cycling, swimming, skipping rope or stepping will significantly improve your overall cardiovascular health. Cardiovascular training is referred to as the ability of the cardiovascular/cardiopulmonary system (heart, lungs, blood vessels) to deliver an adequate supply of oxygen to exercising muscles.

The flow of blood to the muscles increases when performing weight training exercises. For this reason, progressive cardiovascular training will help reduce body fat, increase oxygen and nutrient uptake, improve stress tolerance, and lower your blood pressure. The duration of the exercise can be from 20-30 minutes for high impact and up to 45-60 minutes for low impact aerobics.

By performing an aerobic activity that stimulates a 70 percent target heart rate, over time you will begin to achieve a significant reduction in body fat. In most instances, people involved in aerobics are not aware of this fact. A reduction in body fat can be accomplished by working the cardiovascular system to its full potential. Your 70 percent target heart rate is equal to 220 minus your age, multiplied by 0.7, times 1.15. Increasing your aerobic activity level to a 70 percent target heart rate will stimulate the reduction in body fat you have been striving to achieve. Since your metabolic rate slows down in the evening, to help your metabolism maximize food utilization and minimize fat storage, try to eat your last meal before 8:00 p.m.

Flexibility Training

Flexibility training is often an overlooked component in weight training and is defined as a joint's ability to move freely through a full and normal range of motion. Flexibility training will improve your overall and specific flexibility, as well as prevent injuries.

The following basic information will help you incorporate flexibility training into your weight training program:

1. Perform flexibility training after a 5-10 minute general warm-up and during the cool-down period. Muscles and tendons are more pliable and stretch better following a warm-up.

2. Stretch specific muscles or muscle groups.

3. Performing a slow, passive static stretch is recommended. Static flexibility is defined as the range of motion about a joint, with minimum speed of movement (bouncing).

4. Stretch to the point of maximum tension in the muscle without experiencing pain.

5. Hold each stretch for 15-30 seconds.

6. Perform 3-5 repetitions for each stretch.

2
ABDOMINAL
EXERCISES

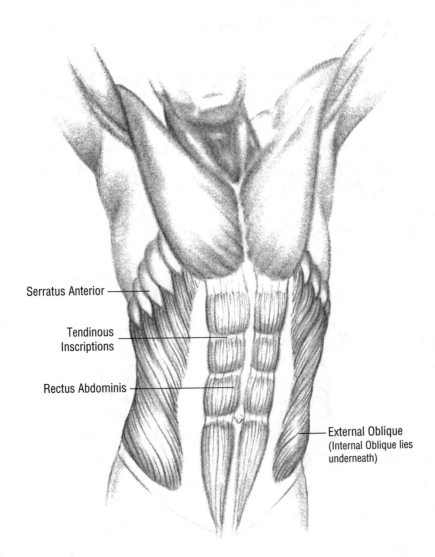

Serratus Anterior

Tendinous
Inscriptions

Rectus Abdominis

External Oblique
(Internal Oblique lies
underneath)

BENT-KNEE
HANGING LEG RAISE

Muscles Involved: The external oblique, rectus abdominis, and rectus femoris.

Execution: Grasp a chinning bar with an overhand grip and hang at arms length.

1. Slowly bend your knees and lift your legs as high as possible; 2. Slowly lower them back to the starting position; 3. Repeat as required.

Important: Bending the knees significantly reduces the resistance. As an advanced exercise, keep your legs straight throughout the movement.

CRUNCHES

Muscles Involved: The rectus abdominis, external oblique and internal oblique (collectively, the abdominals).

Execution: Lie on your back with your legs up in the air and feet crossed. Interlace your hands behind your head or cross them at your chest.

1. Raise your head and shoulders off the floor as high as possible. You will only have a range of motion of approximately 30-45 degrees; 2. Slowly lower yourself to the starting position; 3. Repeat as required at a moderate pace.

Important: Performing crunches with your hands behind your neck may appear easier as the range of motion is smaller. If you want a more intense abdominal workout, place your hands across your chest and touch your elbows to your knees. This method eliminates possible injury to your neck.

FLAT BENCH LEG RAISE

Muscles Involved: The rectus abdominis, external oblique and internal oblique (collectively, the abdominals).

Execution: Lie on your back on a flat exercise bench and extend your legs straight out.

1. Keep your legs straight and and together, and slowly raise them until they are vertical; 2. Slowly lower your legs until they are slightly below bench level; 3. Repeat as required.

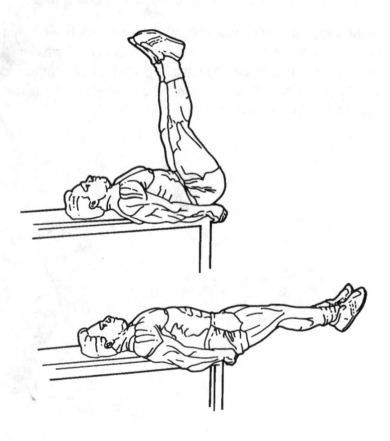

INCLINE SIT-UP

Muscles Involved: The rectus femoris, iliopsoas, pectineus, rectus abdominis, and external oblique.

Execution: Sit on an incline sit-up bench and place your feet under the foot supports. Fold your arms across your chest.

   1. Slowly lower yourself back approximately 70 degrees or until your lower back touches the chair; 2. Slowly raise back up to the starting position; 3. Repeat as required.

Important: To place maximum stress on your abdominals, do not go beyond 90 degrees, or when your torso is parallel to the floor.

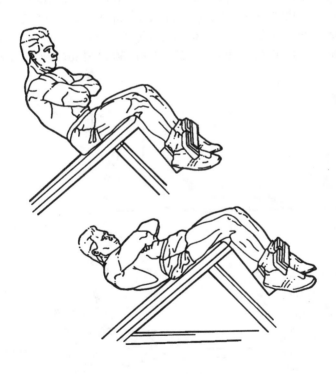

REVERSE CRUNCH

Muscles Involved: The rectus abdominis, external oblique and internal oblique (collectively, the abdominals).

Execution: Lie on your back on an exercise mat or carpeted floor. Place your arms on the floor above your head and raise your thighs, with bent knees, to just above your chest.

1. Keep your feet together and contract your lower abdominal muscles to raise your pelvis up until your hips are off the floor (your knees will be close to your chest); 2. Slowly lower your pelvis back to the starting position; 3. Repeat as required.

Important: Do not let your feet touch the floor during the exercise. To involve your upper abdominal muscles, continue the movement until your knees are close to your chin. This is an advanced movement and not recommended for beginners.

REVERSE TRUNK TWIST

Muscles Involved: The external oblique and internal oblique.

Execution: Lie on your back with your arms straight out from your sides and legs extended straight up from the floor (vertical). If you experience tension in your legs, bend them slightly.

1. Keep your feet together and slowly lower your legs to the left, touching the floor with your outside foot; 2. Slowly raise your legs back to the starting position; 3. Repeat to the opposite side; 4. Repeat as required.

Important: To properly perform this exercise keep your shoulders and arms on the floor at all times. This will provide maximum stretching and strengthening of the internal and external obliques.

ROPE PULL-DOWN

Muscles Involved: The upper rectus abdominis, external oblique, and internal oblique (collectively, the abdominals), latissimus dorsi, teres major, lower pectorals, posterior deltoid, and long head of the triceps.

Execution: Attach a rope to a high pulley or lat pulldown apparatus and kneel in front of the cable holding the rope with a neutral grip. Lean forward until the cable is taut and your arms are bent at the elbows.

1. Slowly pull down with your upper body in a curling motion trying to bring your chest and shoulders to your thighs (at full contraction your elbows will be touching the floor between your knees); 2. Slowly return to the starting position; 3. Repeat as required.

Important: The emphasis during the first half of the movement is on the lats, then the upper abs are worked from the midpoint to full contraction. To achieve a greater range of motion, use a 6-8 inch platform bringing your elbows below the level of the platform.

SEATED KNEE-UP

Muscles Involved: The rectus abdominis, external oblique, and internal oblique (collectively, the abdominals), psoas, iliacus, rectus femoris, and pectineus.

Execution: Sit on an exercise bench with your buttocks close to the end. Place your hands 6-12 inches behind your buttocks grasping the sides of the bench for support. Lean back to a 45-60 degree angle placing your weight on your arms. Extend your legs out until they are level with the floor.

1. Slowly bend your legs and bring your knees toward your chest; 2. When your knees are as close to your chest as possible, straighten your legs and return to the starting position; 3. Repeat as required.

Important: Keep your upper body stabilized and bring your knees as close to your chest as possible to provide greater abdominal development. Support your upper body by keeping your arms straight to reduce the risk of injury.

SIT-UP

Muscles Involved: The upper rectus abdominis, external oblique, and internal oblique.

Execution: Lie back on a sit-up board with your knees slightly flexed and feet firmly secured under the support strap or rollers. Place your hands behind your head or across your chest.

1. Slowly sit up, attempting to touch your elbows to your knees; 2. Without allowing your back to touch the board, slowly lower yourself back to the starting position; 3. Repeat as required.

Important: Do not pull your head forward or perform sit-ups with straight legs since this can lead to neck or lower back problems. As your abs become more developed the sit-up should be modified to increase the difficulty.

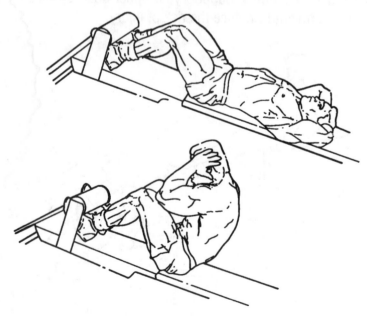

SUPPORT
VERTICAL LEG RAISE

Muscles Involved: The rectus abdominis, external oblique, rectus femoris, iliopsoas, and pectineous.

Execution: Support yourself with your forearms on a standing vertical bench. Position your back firmly against the back pad and let your legs hang fully extended.

1. Keep your upper body steady and slowly bend your knees raising your legs above your waist; 2. Slowly lower your legs back to the starting position; 3. Repeat as required.

Important: To maintain proper form, keep your lower back against the back support at all times. Bending the knees significantly reduces the resistance. As an advanced exercise, keep your legs straight throughout the movement.

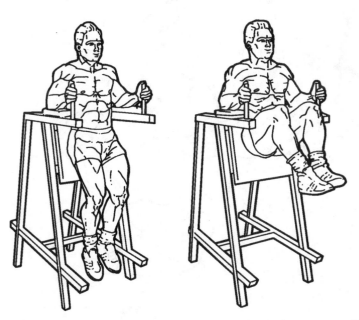

TWISTING CRUNCHES

Muscles Involved: The rectus abdominis, external oblique, and internal oblique (collectively, the abdominals).

Execution: Lie with your back on the floor and clasp your hands loosely behind your head. Bend your knees and raise your legs into the air crossing them at the ankles.

1. Slowly sit up, bringing your left elbow to your right knee;
2. Slowly lower yourself back to the starting position;
3. Slowly sit up, bringing your right elbow to your left knee;
4. Repeat as required.

Important: Do not pull your head forward. This exercise will work a larger part of the abdominal area, including the obliques and intercostals.

3
CHEST
EXERCISES

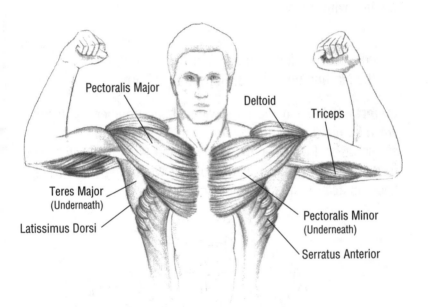

Pectoralis Major

Deltoid

Triceps

Teres Major
(Underneath)

Latissimus Dorsi

Pectoralis Minor
(Underneath)

Serratus Anterior

DIPS

Muscles Involved: The anterior deltoid, upper pectoralis major, pectoralis minor, lower trapezius and rhomboid, and tricep brachii.

Execution: If the dip bars are adjustable, position them shoulder-width or slightly wider than shoulder-width apart. Grasp the bars and jump up to support yourself with arms fully extended and elbows locked. Bend the knees slightly to avoid contact with the floor.

1. Slowly lower your body as far as possible without losing control; 2. Slowly press your body up until you return to the starting position; 3. Repeat as required.

Important: Moving the bars wider than shoulder width apart will minimize the anterior deltoid and triceps, bringing the latissimus dorsi, lower pectoralis major and teres major into play. If you elect to go less than shoulder-width apart, the triceps become heavily stressed.

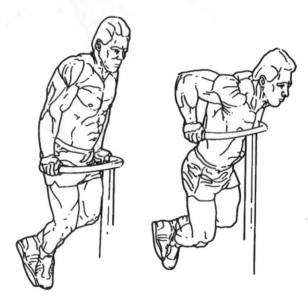

BENCH PRESS

Muscles Involved: The pectoralis major, pectoralis minor, anterior deltoid, and triceps brachii.

Execution: Lie back on the bench with your head under the barbell rack and feet flat on the floor. Grasp the barbell with an overhand grip, hands equally spaced, about shoulder-width apart.

1. Press the barbell off the rack so it is directly above your chest; 2. Slowly bend your elbows, allowing the bar to descend to the middle of your chest; 3. Slowly press the barbell back to the starting position; 4. Repeat as required.

Important: For greater pectoralis major and anterior deltoid development, drop your elbows as far as possible. A spotter is recommended when using maximum weight.

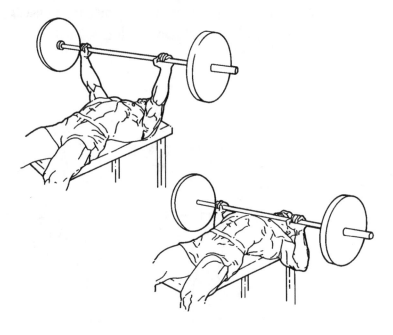

BENT-ARM PULLOVER

Muscles Involved: The lower pectoralis major, latissimus dorsi, and teres major.

Execution: Lie on an exercise bench with your shoulders at the end. Place your feet flat on the floor. Make sure your back and pelvis are stable. Grasp a dumbbell and hold it with both hands supporting it directly over your chest with your palms facing up. Keeping your elbows flexed, slowly lower the dumbbell backwards over your head until your upper arms are directly in line with your body, your forearms vertical.

1. Keep your elbows flexed and slowly raise the dumbbell until your upper arms are perpendicular to the bench;
2. Slowly lower the dumbbell to the starting position;
3. Repeat as required.

Important: Bent-Arm Pullovers will allow you to use significantly more weight. If you position your shoulders crosswise on the bench, <u>do not lower the pelvis below the bench</u>. This can cause possible injury.

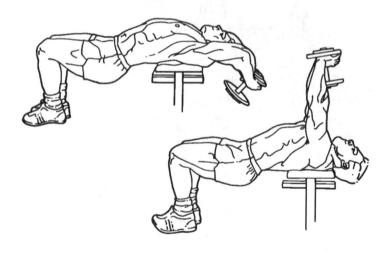

BENT-OVER
CABLE CROSSOVER

Muscles Involved: The pectoralis major, pectoralis minor, serratus anterior, anterior deltoid, and coracobrachhialis.

Execution: Grasp the handles of two crossover overhead pulleys with a palm-down grip. With your feet shoulder-width apart, bend over at the hips keeping your back slightly arched, until your upper body is horizontal to the ground. Pull the handles down until they are in line with your shoulders.

1. Slowly pull the handles downward and inward until they cross in front of your chest; 2. Maintaining control, slowly return to the starting position; 3. Repeat as required.

Important: To maximize development of the inner pectorals, cross your arms as much as possible keeping the wrists firmly in place.

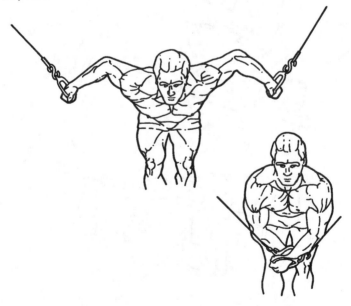

DECLINE BENCH PRESS

Muscles Involved: The lower pectoralis major, pectoralis minor, anterior deltoid, and serratus anterior.

Execution: Lie back on the bench with your head at the lower end and knees over the edge, feet secure under the pads. In this position, grasp the bar with an evenly spaced, shoulder-width overhand grip.

1. Press the barbell off the rack so it is directly above your chest; 2. Slowly lower the barbell until it touches your lower chest; 3. Slowly press the barbell back to the starting position; 4. Repeat as required.

DUMBBELL FLYE

Muscles Involved: The pectoralis major, pectoralis minor, anterior deltoid, coracobrachialis, and serratus anterior.

Execution: Grasp a dumbbell in each hand with an over-hand grip and lie back on an exercise bench with your feet flat on the floor. The spine, head, and buttocks should make full contact with the bench. Press the dumbbells above your chest so the arms are fully extended, palms facing each other.

1. Keeping the arms extended, bend slightly at the elbows and slowly move the dumbbells out to your sides in an arc to shoulder level or slightly below; 2. Following the same arc, return the dumbbells to the starting position; 3. Repeat as required.

Important: Do not use excessively heavy weights. Heavy weights will prevent you from performing the exercise correctly and you will not achieve desired results. When performed correctly, the dumbbell flye is one of the best exercises to develop the middle pectoralis major muscles.

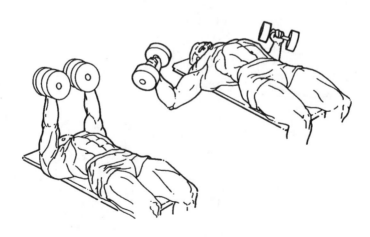

DUMBBELL PULLOVER

Muscles Involved: The lower pectoralis major, latissimus dorsi, teres major, rhomboid, and pectoralis minor.

Execution: Grasp a dumbbell and lie on your back on an exercise bench with your shoulders at the end. Place your feet flat on the floor. Hold the dumbbell with both hands supporting it directly over your chest, palms facing up. Slightly bend your elbows, but keep them relatively straight throughout the movement.

1. Slowly lower the dumbbell backwards over your head until your upper arms are directly in line with or slightly below the bench; 2. Slowly raise (pullover) the dumbbell to the starting position; 3. Repeat as required.

Important: To receive maximum ribcage expansion, keep your arms as straight as possible. Bend the elbows further if you experience a great deal of stress.

INCLINE BENCH PRESS

Muscles Involved: The anterior deltoid, upper pectoralis major, pectoralis minor, serratus anterior, and triceps brachii.

Execution: Grasp two dumbbells with an overhand grip and lie back on a 45-degree incline bench with your feet flat on the floor. Press the dumbbells up until they are directly above your chest with your arms fully extended and elbows locked.

1. Slowly lower the dumbbells until they are at or slightly below chest level; 2. Slowly press the dumbbells back to the starting position; 3. Repeat as required.

Important: It is recommended that you have a spotter when performing this exercise with extra heavy weights.

INCLINE
DUMBBELL FLYE√

Muscles Involved: The pectorails major, pectoralis minor, serratus anterior, coracobrachialis, and anterior deltoid.

Execution: Lie back on an incline bench with your feet flat on the floor. Grasp two dumbbells with an overhand grip and hold them with your arms fully extended above your chest, palms facing each other.

1. Slowly move the dumbbells out to your sides in an arc to the lowest possible point, bending slightly at the elbows; 2. Following the same arc, return the dumbbells to the starting position; 3. Repeat as required.

Important: To maintain proper form, avoid bringing the weights in close to your body or pressing them straight up.

4

TRICEP EXERCISES

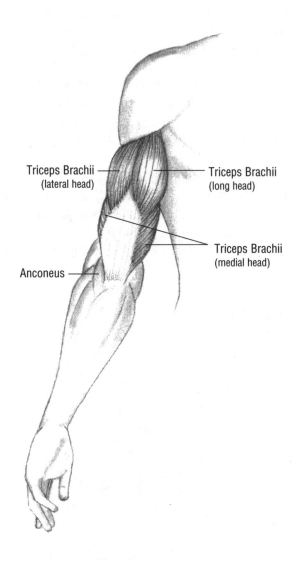

Triceps Brachii
(lateral head)

Triceps Brachii
(long head)

Triceps Brachii
(medial head)

Anconeus

Muscles Involved: The triceps lateral head, long head, and medial head (collectively, the triceps), and anconeus.

Execution: Lie lengthwise on an exercise bench with your head slightly extended over one end. Hold a dumbbell with both hands extended at a 45-degree angle to the bench.

1. Keep your upper arms and elbows stationary. Bend at the elbows, lowering your forearms until they are perpendicular to the floor; 2. Slowly extend your forearms back up to the 45-degree starting position; 3. Repeat as required.

Important: Keeping your upper arms and elbows stationary will produce a greater stretch in the triceps, thus producing a more powerful contraction. For maximum development you must lock out your elbows at the end of the movement. This exercise can also be performed using a short barbell or EZ-curl bar.

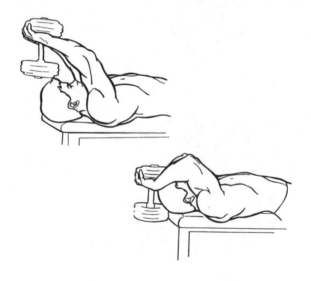

BEHIND-THE-BACK DIPS

Muscles Involved: The triceps lateral head, long head, and medial head (collectively, the triceps).

Execution: Place two flat exercise benches parallel to each other about 3-4 feet apart. With your hands shoulder-width apart and arms fully extended, hold on to the edge of one bench and place your heels on the other.

1. Slowly bend your elbows, lowering your body as close to the floor as possible without touching it; 2. Slowly push your body back up to the starting position; 3. Repeat as required.

Important: To increase the intensity of the movement, place a weight plate across your lap.

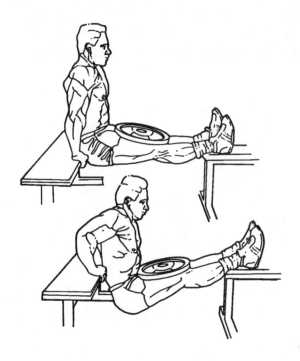

DUMBBELL KICKBACK

Muscles Involved: The triceps lateral head, long head, and medial head (collectively, the triceps).

Execution: Grasp a dumbbell and support yourself on an exercise bench with your knee and free hand. Hold the dumbbell keeping your upper arm and elbow in line with and against your upper body with your forearm hanging straight down.

1. Keep your upper arm in place and extend your forearm to the rear until it is straight; 2. Continue this movement as far as possible after the arm is fully extended and until the dumbbell is slightly above your back; 3. Slowly return the dumbbell to the starting position; 4. Repeat as required.

Important: To keep your back in the horizontal position throughout this exercise place your free hand on a sufficiently low bench. If you cannot perform the exercise with proper form it will be necessary to reduce the amount of weight used.

LYING CROSS FACE
TRICEPS EXTENSION

Muscles Involved: The triceps lateral head, long head, and medial head (collectively, the triceps).

Execution: Grasp a dumbbell and lie on your back on a flat exercise bench with your head close to the end, your knees bent and feet flat on the floor. Hold the dumbbell in your left hand at arms length above your head.

1. Keep your upper arm stationary and slowly lower the dumbbell across your face until it touches your right shoulder; 2. Slowly extend your arm, returning to the starting position; 3. Repeat as required, then perform the same number of reps with the opposite arm.

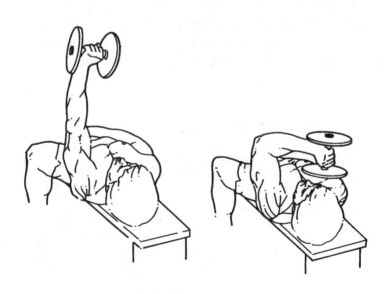

LYING
TRICEPS EXTENSION √

Muscles Involved: The triceps lateral head, long head, and medial head (collectively, the triceps).

Execution: Grasp a barbell with a narrow overhand grip (six inches or less between hands) and lie back on an exercise bench with your head at one end and feet flat on the floor. Press the bar until it is directly above your head with your palms facing toward your feet.

1. Keep your upper arms stationary and slowly lower the barbell in a semicircle until it is behind your head; 2. Slowly return the barbell along the same arc to the starting position; 3. Repeat as required.

Important: To work your triceps effectively you must use a narrow grip. This will allow you to work through a greater range of motion. It is recommended that you have a spotter when performing this exercise with extra heavy weights.

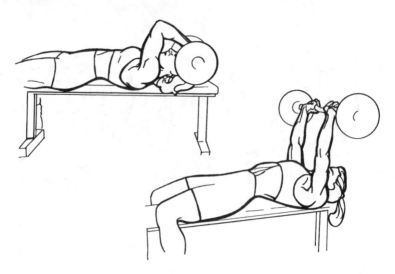

ONE-ARM
TRICEPS EXTENSION ✓

Muscles Involved: The triceps lateral head, long head, and medial head (collectively, the triceps).

Execution: Grasp a dumbbell and sit on the end of a flat exercise bench. Hold the dumbbell at arms length overhead with palm facing forward. Pull your elbow in close to your head and keep your upper arm stationary.

1. Slowly lower the dumbbell in an arc behind your head (not shoulder) as far as possible; 2. Slowly extend your arm, returning the dumbbell to the starting position; 3. Repeat as required, then perform the same number of reps with the opposite arm.

Important: To achieve maximum results, perform this movement with strict form.

REVERSE-GRIP
TRICEPS PUSHDOWN

Muscles Involved: The triceps brachii with emphasis on the lateral head and anconeus.

Execution: Stand in front of a high pulley with your feet shoulder width apart. Grasp the high pulley handle and stand back bending slightly at the hips. Hold the handle so your upper arm and elbow are vertical slightly in front of your body with a 90-degree bend in your elbow.

1. Slowly push down the handle until your arm is fully extended behind you; 2. Slowly return the handle to the starting position; 3. Repeat as required, then perform the same number of reps with the opposite arm.

Important: To achieve maximum results, perform this movement with strict form keeping your upper arm and elbow in place. To develop only the lateral head keep your upper arm and elbow in place alongside your body throughout the movement.

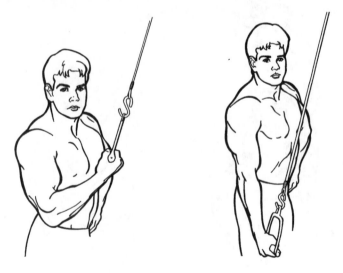

SEATED
TRICEPS EXTENSION

Muscles Involved: The triceps lateral head, long head, and medial head (collectively, the triceps), and anconeus.

Execution: Grasp a barbell with an overhand grip, placing your hands 4-6 inches apart, and sit on the end of an exercise bench. Raise the barbell to arms length over your head, pulling your elbows in close to your head.

1. Keep your upper arms stationary and slowly lower the barbell in an arc behind your head as far as possible;
2. Slowly press the barbell back to the starting position;
3. Repeat as required.

Important: This exercise can be performed using a straight bar or E-Z curl bar on an incline or decline bench. Triceps extensions can also be performed in a standing position.

TRICEP PUSHDOWN √

Muscles Involved: The triceps lateral head, long head, and medial head (collectively, the triceps).

Execution: Stand close to an overhead pulley cable and grasp the bar with an overhand grip, hands 6-10 inches apart. Pull your el-bows in close to your body and keep your body erect.

1. Slowly press the bar down as far as possible, locking your elbows; 2. Slowly return the bar to the middle of your chest; 3. Repeat as required.

Important: This exercise can be performed using a variety of techniques. For example, you can vary your grip, type of bar used, width between your hands, and distance of the movement.

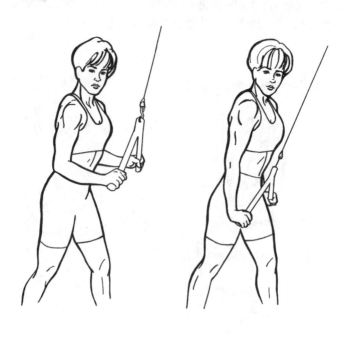

5
BICEP
EXERCISES

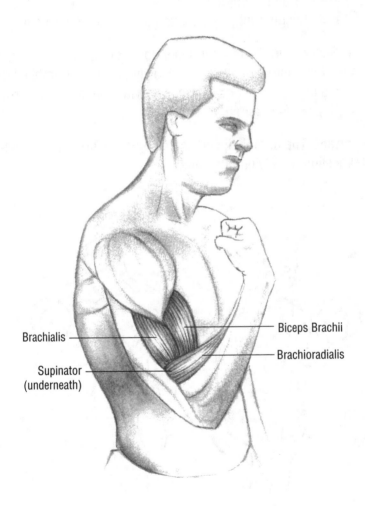

Brachialis

Supinator
(underneath)

Biceps Brachii

Brachioradialis

ALTERNATE DUMBBELL CURL

Muscles Involved: The biceps brachii, brachialis, and brachio-radialis (collectively, the biceps), and supinator.

Execution: Stand upright holding a dumbbell in each hand, your arms hanging fully extended, palms facing your body.

1. Slowly curl the left dumbbell up as far as possible while twisting your palm inward; 2. Slowly lower the dumbbell to the starting position; 3. Repeat with the opposite arm; 4. Repeat as required, alternating arms.

Important: The dumbbell curl can also be performed in a seated, kneeling, and lying position.

CONCENTRATION CURL ✓

Muscles Involved: The biceps brachii, brachialis, and brachio-radialis (collectively, the biceps).

Execution: Grasp a dumbbell and bend over slightly allowing the dumbbell to hang at arms length. Place your free hand on your knee or stationary object for support.

1. Slowly curl the dumbbell up to your shoulder. As you reach your shoulder, twist the dumbbell so your thumb is lower than your little finger; 2. Slowly lower the dumbbell to the starting position; 3. Repeat as required, then perform the same number of reps with the opposite arm.

HAMMER CURL ✓

Muscles Involved: The biceps brachii, brachialis, and brachio-radialis (collectively, the biceps).

Execution: Grasp two dumbbells and sit on the end of a flat exercise bench with your arms hanging fully extended from your sides, palms facing your body. Keeping your upper arms stationary.

1. Slowly curl the dumbbells up until their ends touch your shoulders; 2. Slowly lower the dumbbells back to the starting position; 3. Repeat as required.

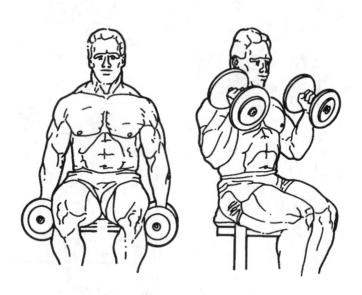

INCLINE BICEPS CURL ✓

Muscles Involved: The biceps brachii, brachialis, and brachioradialis (collectively, the biceps), and supinator.

Execution: Grasp a dumbbell in each hand and either sit on an incline bench or stand on an incline board with your head and upper body in full contact with the pad. Your arms will hang fully extended from your sides, palms facing your body.

1. Slowly curl the dumbbells up to your shoulders keeping the elbows pointed straight down; 2. Slowly lower the dumbbells to the starting position; 3. Repeat as required.

Important: For full involvement of the biceps, turn the weight outward so your palms face up and back when they reach your shoulders.

PREACHER CURL ✓

Muscles Involved: The biceps brachii, brachialis, and brachio-radialis (collectively, the biceps).

Execution: Lean over the preacher curl bench and grasp the barbell with an underhand grip, hands evenly spaced, shoulder-width apart. Sit into the bench, wedging your armpits over the top of the pad and run your upper arms down the surface of the bench. Allow your arms to straighten out completely.

1. Slowly curl the barbell up until it reaches the base of your throat; 2. Slowly lower the barbell until it reaches the starting position or until the arms are fully extended; 3. Repeat as required.

Important: To vary the intensity of this exercise, change your grip from very narrow to as wide as the bar permits. This movement can be performed with an E-Z curl bar or with dumbbells using alternate arms.

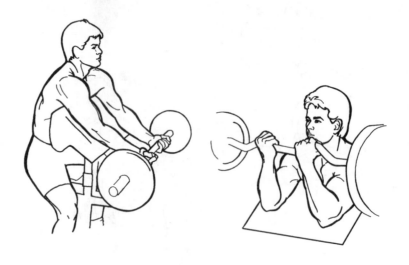

PULLEY CURL

Muscles Involved: The biceps brachii, brachialis, and brachio-radialis (collectively, the biceps).

Execution: Attach a curl bar to the cable running through a floor pulley and grasp the bar with a narrow underhand grip. Stand back from the floor pulley with your feet shoulder-width apart, arms straight and upper arms tight against the body.

1. Slowly curl the bar from the starting position until it reaches a point just under the chin; 2. Slowly allow the bar to return to the starting position; 3. Repeat as required.

Important: This exercise can also be performed one arm at a time with a loop handle attached to the pulley cable.

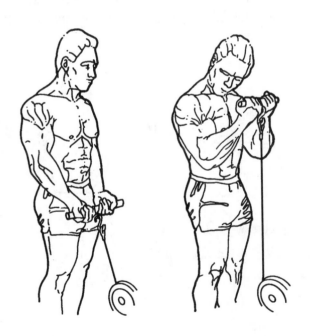

REVERSE BICEPS CURL

Muscles Involved: The biceps brachii, brachialis, and brachio-radialis (collectively, the biceps).

Execution: Grasp a barbell with an over-hand grip and assume a standing position with your feet and hands shoulder width apart. Allow the barbell to rest against your thighs with your elbows touching the sides of your body.

1. Slowly curl the barbell in a semicircle to the top of your chest; 2. Slowly lower the barbell along the same arc to the starting position; 3. Repeat as required.

Important: To place greater stress on the biceps use a narrower grip. Because of increased difficulty with a narrower grip, less weight will be required. To isolate your forearms and increase the intensity of this movement, perform it on a preacher curl bench.

6
FOREARM
EXERCISES

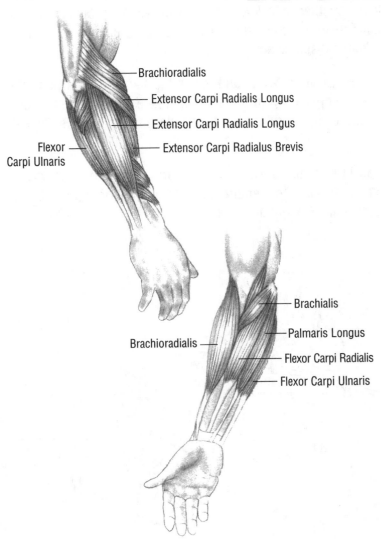

Brachioradialis

Extensor Carpi Radialis Longus

Extensor Carpi Radialis Longus

Flexor Carpi Ulnaris

Extensor Carpi Radialus Brevis

Brachialis

Palmaris Longus

Brachioradialis

Flexor Carpi Radialis

Flexor Carpi Ulnaris

BARBELL WRIST CURL

Muscles Involved: The flexor carpi radialis and flexor carpi ulnaris.

Execution: Grasp a barbell with an underhand grip, hands close together, and kneel next to an exercise bench resting your forearms across thebench. Keep your elbows and wrists the same distance apart.

1.Relax your wrists and lower the bar as far as possible while opening your fingers to increase the range of motion; 2. Slowly return the bar to the starting position; 3. Repeat as required.

Important: Your forearm muscles are similar to your calves and abs in that they require a greater degree of stimulation to increase in strength and size.

ONE-ARM
DUMBBELL WRIST CURL

Muscles Involved: The flexor carpi radials and flexor carpi ulnaris.

Execution: Grasp a dumbbell and sit on the end of an exercise bench. Lean forward, placing your forearm on your thigh so your wrist and dumbbell are clear of your knee. Stabilize your elbow with your free hand.

1. Relax your wrist, slowly lowering the dumbbell as far as possible toward the floor, while opening your fingers slightly to increase the range of motion; 2. Slowly curl the dumbbell back to the starting position; 3. Repeat as required, then perform the same number of reps with the other arm.

RADIAL FLEXION

Muscles Involved: The extensor carpi radialis and flexor carpi radialis.

Execution: Stand with your feet shoulder-width apart holding a strength bar by the open end with the weight in front of you. Relax your wrist muscles and allow the bar to hang at its lowest point in front of your body.

1. Keep your arm straight and slowly flex your wrist raising the weighted end of the bar up as high as possible; 2. Slowly lower the bar to the starting position; 3. Repeat as required.

Important: To achieve maximum efficiency, always keep your arm straight, grip the bar a maximum of 15 inches from the weight, use only your wrist, and raise the weight as high as possible.

REVERSE WRIST CURL

Muscles Involved: The extensor carpi radialis longus, extensor carpi radialis brevis, and extensor carpi ulnaris.

Execution: Grasp the barbell or dumbbell with an overhand grip, palms facing down and kneel in front of and place your forearms across an exercise bench so your hands extend beyond the far side. Lower your hands as far as possible.

1. Slowly raise your hand(s) as high as possible or until they are perpendicular with the forearms; 2. Slowly lower to the starting position; 3. Repeat as required.

Important: The amount of weight used will regulate your range of motion. This exercise can also be performed with dumbbells.

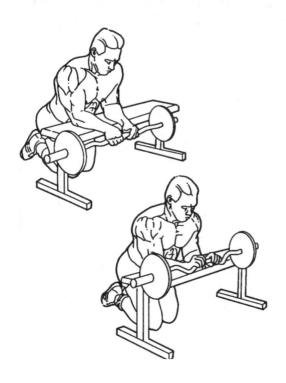

ULNAR FLEXION

Muscles Involved: The extensor carpi ulnaris and flexor carpi ulnaris.

Execution: Stand with your feet shoulder-width apart holding a strength bar by the open end with the weight behind you. Relax your wrist muscles and allow the bar to hang at its lowest point behind your body.

1. Keep your arm straight and slowly flex your wrist raising the weighted end of the bar up as high as possible; 2. Slowly lower the bar to the starting position; 3. Repeat as required.

Important: To achieve maximum efficiency, always keep your arm straight. Grip the bar a maximum of 15 inches from the weight, use only your wrist and raise the weight as high as possible.

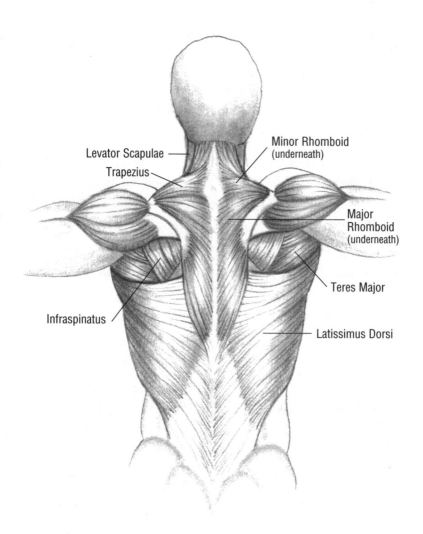

Levator Scapulae

Trapezius

Minor Rhomboid
(underneath)

Major
Rhomboid
(underneath)

Teres Major

Infraspinatus

Latissimus Dorsi

BACK RAISE

Muscles Involved: The iliocostalis thoracis, iliocostalis lumborum, longissimus dorsi and spinalis dorsi (collectively, the erector spinae muscle group), and intertransversarii, interspinalis, rotatores, and multifidus muscles (collectively, the deep spinal muscle group).

Execution: Lie face-down on a hyperextension bench with your feet under the rear foot support and hips on top of the seat. Your navel should be no further than the edge of the seat. Hang over the seat at approximately a 45-60 degree angle. Cross your arms over your chest or place then loosely behind your head.

1. Slowly raise your upper body until it is straight or slightly higher (your back should be slightly arched); 2. Slowly relax and return to the starting position; 3. Repeat as required.

Important: Perform the Back Raise slowly and smoothly without jerking or using your momentum to raise your upper body.

BENT-OVER BARBELL ROW

Muscles Involved: The posterior deltoid, teres minor, trapezius, rhomboid major, and rhomboid minor.

Execution: Stand with your feet a few inches apart and grasp a barbell with a wide overhand grip. With your knees bent slightly, bend over at the hips until your upper body is parallel with the floor. Keep your back straight or slightly arched and allow the barbell to hang at arms length.

1. Vigorously pull the barbell up until it touches your chest;
2. Slowly lower the barbell back to the starting position;
3. Repeat as required.

Important: To ensure proper development of the lats, always keep your back parallel to the floor and pull the barbell up so that your elbows are higher than the level of your back. Otherwise you will be including the lower back and arms in the movement. Too narrow of a grip will limit your range of motion.

BENT-OVER DUMBBELL ROW √

Muscles Involved: The lower latissimus dorsi, lower pectoralis major, pectoralis minor, teres major, rhomboid, and middle fibers of the trapezius.

Execution: Grasp a dumbbell with an overhand grip and assume a bent-over position with your arm fully extended alongside an exercise bench. Bend at the hips and support yourself by placing the hand and leg closest to the bench on the bench. Keep your back flat and leg slightly bent. Your back should be level with the floor from hips to neck.

1. Slowly pull the dumbbell up keeping your elbow out to the side and your upper arm in line with your shoulders. At the top your elbow should be higher than your back; 2. Slowly return to the starting position; 3. Repeat as required, then perform the same number of reps with the other arm.

Important: To ensure proper technique it is important to keep your upper body stationary while in the bent-over position.

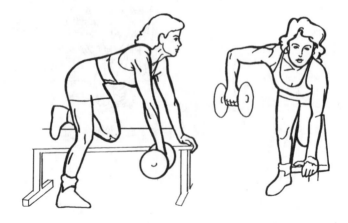

LAT PULLDOWN ✓

Muscles Involved: The lower pectoralis major, pectoralis minor, latissimus dorsi, teres major, and rhomboid.

Execution: Grasp the bar of a lat pulldown with a wider than shoulder-width overhand grip. With your hands equally spaced, sit placing your legs under the padded braces.

1. Slowly pull the bar down until it touches the top of your chest; 2. Slowly allow the bar to return to the starting position; 3. Repeat as required.

Important: Maintaining strict form will ensure greater back development. Do not sway back when pulling the bar down as this will bring the lower back into the movement. For variation, perform the lat pulldown to the back of your neck.

NARROW GRIP ✓
LAT PULLDOWN

Muscles Involved: The pectoralis major, latissimus dorsi, middle trapezius, teres major, triceps, pectoralis minor, posterior deltoid, and rhomboid.

Execution: Grasp the narrow grip handles and sit with your upper legs under the thigh pads of a lat pulldown machine. Your arms will be fully extended with your palms facing each other.

1. Keeping your upper body erect throughout the movement, slowly pull the handles down to your upper chest;
2. Slowly allow handles to return to the starting position;
3. Repeat as required.

Important: Keeping your body erect throughout the movement will work both the upper and lower latissimus dorsi. To isolate the lower latissimus dorsi, lean back while performing the movement. The further you lean back, the greater stress you place on the lower lats. When leaning back, be sure to pull the handles toward your upper abs.

SEATED
PULLEY ROWING

Muscles Involved: The middle trapezius, medial and posterior deltoid, teres minor, infraspinatus, and rhomboid.

Execution: Sit down at a low cable pulley with your feet braced at the foot bar or metal plate so that your body will remain in place. Grasp the bar with a palms-down grip or handles with palms facing together. Your trunk should be perpendicular to the floor and arms outstretched making the cable taut.

1. Pull toward your chest keeping the elbows moving back and to the sides as far as possible; 2. Slowly allow your arms to return to the starting position; 3. Repeat as required.

Important: Your back must remain stationary throughout this exercise to ensure proper technique and correct muscle involvement.

SHOULDER SHRUG

Muscles Involved: The upper trapezius, levator scapulae, and rhomboid.

Execution: Stand with your feet shoulder-width apart. Hold a dumbbell in each hand with the shaft forward-rearward. Keep your head stationary and chin slightly down by focusing on a spot in front of you.

1. Keep your shoulders back and chest out. Slowly raise your shoulders up as high as possible; 2. Slowly lower your shoulders down as far as possible; 3. Repeat as required.

T-BAR
BENT-OVER ROW

Muscles Involved: The posterior deltoid, teres minor, trapezius, rhomboid major, and rhomboid minor.

Execution: Position yourself on the T-bar apparatus and bend at the hips keeping your trunk straight and firm. Place your feet shoulder-width apart with knees slightly bent. Grasp the T-bar handles with a wide overhand grip.

1. Vigorously pull the T-bar up to your chest keeping your elbows out to the sides and upper arms perpendicular to your trunk (your back should remain straight or slightly arched); 2. Slowly lower the T-bar to the starting position; 3. Repeat as required.

Important: To ensure proper development of the lats, always keep your back parallel to the floor and pull the barbell up so that your elbows are higher than the level of your back. Otherwise, you will be including the lower back and arms in the movement. Too narrow of a grip will limit your range of motion. The use of a weight lifting belt is recommended.

WIDE-GRIP CHIN-UP

Muscles Involved: The teres major, latissimus dorsi, pectoralis major, the biceps brachii, brachialis, and brachioradialis (collectively, the biceps), and pectoralis minor.

Execution: Jump up and grasp a chinning bar with an over-hand grip, hands as wide as possible. Hang from the bar with your knees bent and ankles crossed to prevent touching the floor.

1. Slowly pull yourself up until your chin is at or above the bar; 2. Slowly return to the starting position; 3. Repeat as required.

Important: Performing wide grip chins for the first time will normally be difficult thus limiting the number of reps. If you have a training partner have him or her help you with a few forced reps when you can no longer complete your set. For a greater range of motion, pull up so the bar touches your upper chest rather than the back of your neck.

8
SHOULDER
EXERCISES

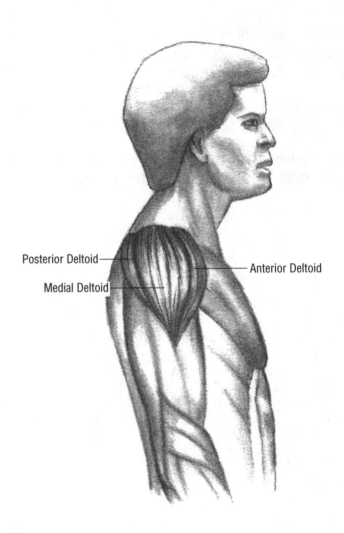

Posterior Deltoid

Medial Deltoid

Anterior Deltoid

BEHIND-THE-NECK PRESS

Muscles Involved: The middle and anterior deltoids, supraspinatus, pectoralis minor, serratus anterior, triceps brachii, and trapezius.

Execution: Sit into a smith press or shoulder press bench and grasp the bar with an overhand grip, hands slightly more than shoulder-width apart. Bring the bar to shoulder level behind your neck, keeping the elbows to the outside and upper arms perpendicular to the body.

1. Slowly press the bar up until your elbows lock; 2. Slowly return to the starting position; 3. Repeat as required.

Important: Performing this movement in a seated position will increase the strictness and intensity of the movement.

BENT-OVER
CABLE LATERAL RAISE

Muscles Involved: The middle and posterior deltoid, infra-spinatus, teres minor, trapezius, and rhomboid.

Execution: Grasp a low pulley handle in each opposite hand with your palms facing together. Bend over at the hips keeping your back slightly arched and parallel to the floor. Bend your knees slightly for better balance. Allow your arms to hang straight down.

1. Keep your arms straight or slightly bent and in line with your shoulders; 2. Slowly raise the handles out to your sides as high as possible; 3. Slowly return the handles to the start-ing position; 4. Repeat as required.

Important: Bent-over cable laterals are a safe and effective exercise only if you keep your back in its normal, slightly arched position. Rounding your back can produce severe stress and cause injury.

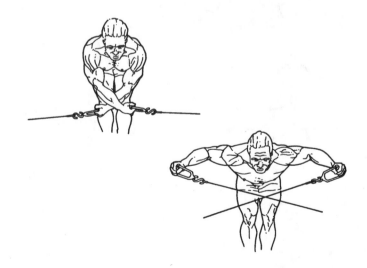

DUMBBELL PRESS ✓

Muscles Involved: The anterior deltoid, upper pectoralis major, pectoralis minor, supraspinatus, serratus anterior, trapezius, and triceps brachii.

Execution: Grasp two dumbbells and sit on the end of an exercise bench. Hold the dumbbells at shoulder height with arms bent at a 90-degree angle and palms facing forward.

1. Keep your back straight and slowly press both dumbbells overhead until they touch at the top; 2. Slowly lower the dumbbells to the starting position; 3. Repeat as required.

Important: The use of dumbbells will allow you to raise and lower them through a greater range of motion. Less weight is required since each arm is lifting independently of the other.

FRONT ARM RAISE ✓

Muscles Involved: The anterior deltoid, upper pectoralis major, pectoralis minor, coracobrachialis, trapezius, and serratus anterior.

Execution: Stand with your feet shoulder-width apart and toes pointed straight ahead. Grasp two dumbbells with an overhand grip. Relax your arms, allowing the dumbbells to rest across your upper thighs. Keep your spine erect in its normal position.

1. Keep your arms straight and slowly raise the left dumbbell up and forward until it is 45-degrees above shoulder level; 2. Hold this position for a moment; 3. Slowly lower the dumbbell back to the starting position; 4. Repeat with the opposite arm; 5. Repeat as required.

Important: It is not necessary to use heavy weights when performing this exercise because straight arms with slightly bent elbows will produce a greater workload. Performing this exercise in a seated position will provide a stricter movement. This exercise can also be performed with a barbell or low pulley.

INCLINE
LATERAL ARM RAISE

Muscles Involved: The anterior and medial deltoid, supraspinatus, upper and lower trapezius, and serratus anterior.

Execution: Lie sideways on an incline bench with a dumbbell in your hand resting on your hip.

1. Keep your arm straight and slowly raise the dumbbell up until it is nearly above your head; 2. Slowly lower the dumbbell back to the starting position; 4. Repeat as required and then perform the same number of reps with the opposite arm.

Important: Holding the dumbbell with the thumb pointing downward will work the posterior deltoid; with the thumb pointing straight will work the middle deltoid; and with the thumb pointing upward will work the anterior deltoid. For maximum effectiveness, do not use heavy weights. To increase the intensity of the movement, lower the angle of the bench.

OVERHEAD PRESS

Muscles Involved: The anterior deltoid, upper pectoralis major, pectoralic minor, coracobrachialis, serratus anterior, triceps brachii, and trapezius.

Execution: Sit into a overhead bench press and adjust the seat to place the barbell in front of your chest. Grasp the bar with an overhand grip. Press the bar up and off the rack until your arms are fully extended above your head.

1. Slowly lower the bar until it reaches the top of your chest; 2. Maintaining control, slowly raise the bar to the starting position; 3. Repeat as required.

Important: Performing the overhead press in a seated overhead bench press will increase the strictness and intensity of the movement. Keeps your wrists slightly hyperextended for better support. The use of a weight lifting belt is recommended.

PRONE LATERAL RAISE ✓

Muscles Involved: The medial and posterior deltoid, infraspinatus, teres minor, trapezius, and rhomboid.

Execution: With a dumbbell in each hand, lie face-down on a narrow exercise bench with your feet firmly planted on the floor, legs slightly bent. Hold the dumbbells with palms facing inward.

1. Keep the elbows slightly bent and raise your arms sideways to slightly higher than shoulder height; 2. Slowly allow the dumbbells to return to the starting position; 3. Repeat as required.

Important: The prone lateral raise is one of the best exercises for posterior deltoid development. The major element in the performance of this exercise is the height of the elbow. The higher the elbow, the greater the muscle is worked.

SIDE LATERAL ARM RAISE

Muscles Involved: The anterior, middle, and posterior deltoid and supraspinatus.

Execution: Stand with your feet shoulder-width apart holding a dumbbell in each hand, palms facing your body.

1. Bend your elbows slightly and slowly raise the dumbbells sideward and upward until they are above shoulder level; 2. Slowly lower the dumbbells to the starting position; 3. Repeat as required.

Important: This exercise should be performed with strict form and light weight. Side lateral arm raises can also be performed seated on an exercise bench.

UPRIGHT ROW ✓

Muscles Involved: The medial deltoid, supraspinatus, pectoralis major (when the arm is above horizontal), trapezius, serratus anterior, and long head of the biceps brachii.

Execution: Stand with feet shoulder-width apart holding a barbell with an overhand grip, your hands 6-8 inches apart. Allow your arms to hang fully extended with the barbell resting across your upper thighs.

1. Keep your back straight and slowly lift the barbell up keeping it close to your body until it reaches your chin. Your elbows should be up and pointing out at a 30-40 degree angle; 2. Slowly lower the bar back to the starting position; 3. Repeat as required.

Important: This exercise can also be performed with a low pulley using the same technique.

9
LEG
EXERCISES

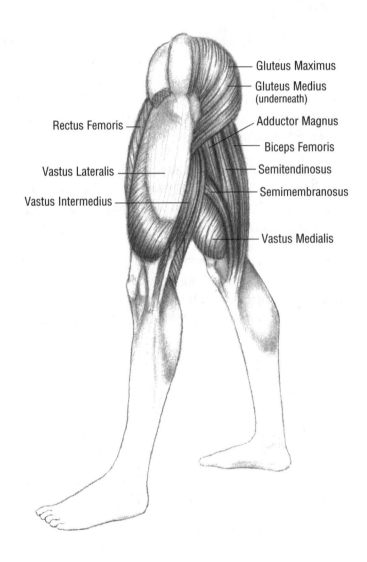

Gluteus Maximus

Gluteus Medius
(underneath)

Rectus Femoris

Adductor Magnus

Biceps Femoris

Vastus Lateralis

Semitendinosus

Vastus Intermedius

Semimembranosus

Vastus Medialis

DEADLIFT

Muscles Involved: The vastus lateralis, vastus medialis, vastus intermedius, rectus femoris (collectively, the quadriceps femoris muscle group); biceps femoris, semitendinosus, semi-membranosus (collectively, the upper hamstrings); and gluteus maximus.

Execution: Assume a position standing next to a barbell on the floor. Bend over at the hips and knees until your pelvic girdle is approximately knee level. In this position, your back should be straight and at a 45-degree angle to the floor. Keeping your arms straight, grasp the bar with a slightly wider than shoulder-width overhand grip.

1. Slowly raise your body by extending your knees and hips until you are fully erect (there should be a slight arch in your back); 2. Slowly lower the barbell back to the floor; 3. Repeat as required.

Important: If you experience difficulty keeping your grip, try using a mixed grip (underhand/overhand). To ensure all-around development, vary the position of your feet. For example, perform the exercise with narrow, regular, and wide stances.

FRONT SQUAT

Muscles Involved: The vastus lateralis, vastus medialis, vastus intermedius, rectus femoris (collectively, the quadriceps femoris muscle group); biceps femoris, semitendinosus, semimembranosus (collectively, the upper hamstrings); and gluteus maximus.

Execution: Assume a standing position with your feet shoulder-width apart and turned slightly to the sides. Grasp the bar with your hands slightly wider than shoulder-width and your elbows up high. Rest the full weight of the bar across your shoulders and upper chest. Keep your head erect or slightly tilted upward.

1. Keep your elbows up and your trunk upright and slowly lower yourself until your thighs are parallel to the floor or slightly below; 2. From this position, slowly push yourself up to the starting position; 3. Repeat as required.

Important: The front squat is more difficult than the squat because of position and balancing. You will find it necessary to use less weight than the squat, especially when first performing this exercise.

GOOD MORNING

Muscles Involved: The biceps femoris, semitendinosus, and semimembranosus (collectively, the upper hamstrings), iliocostalis thoracis, iliocostalis lumborum, longissimus dorsi and spinalis dorsi (collectively, the erector spinae muscle group), intertransversarii, interspinalis, rotatores, and multifidus muscles (collectively, the deep spinal muscle group)and gluteus maximus.

Execution: Grasp a barbell with a wide grip and place it across your shoulders. Stand with your feet shoulder-width apart keeping your legs and back straight.

1. Slowly bend forward from the hips keeping your head up until your upper body is parallel with the floor; 2. Using only your hips, slowly return to the starting position; 3. Repeat as required.

Important: When performing this exercise for the first time, use bent knees and light weight or none at all. Use straight legs only as an advanced exercise.

HACK SQUAT ✓

Muscles Involved: The vastus lateralis, vastus medialis, vastus intermedius, rectus femoris (collectively, the quadriceps femoris muscle group); biceps femoris, semitendinosus, and semimembranosus (collectively, the upper hamstrings); and the gluteus maximus.

Execution: Facing away from the apparatus, position your feet on the inclined platform and rest your shoulders under the pads. Place your back firmly against the back support with your feet together.

1. Press the shoulder pads up until your legs are fully extended and release the safety catch; 2. Bend your knees and slowly lower yourself until there is a 90-degree angle between the knees and hips; 3. Forcefully straighten your legs and return to the starting position; 4. Repeat as required.

Important: To prevent possible injury, keep your feet slightly in front of your body. Placing your feet under your hips can cause severe knee injury.

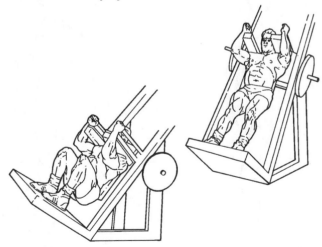

LEG (HIP) ABDUCTION

Muscles Involved: The gluteus medius.

Execution: Attach an ankle strap to your outside leg and stand next to a low pulley station. Attach the strap to the low pulley cable and bring your leg crossed in front of and close to your support leg. With the cable taut, grasp the low pulley apparatus for support.

1. Keep your strapped leg straight, toes facing forward and slowly raise your leg to the side as high as possible (approximately 45-60 degrees); 2. Slowly return your leg to the starting position; 3. Repeat as required.

Important: During the movement, do not turn your toes to the outside (up). Leg abduction can be performed lying on your side with ankle or foot weights or in the standing position using a low pulley.

LEG ADDUCTION

Muscles Involved: The pectineus, gracilis, and the adductors longus, magnus, and brevis.

Execution: Sit into the leg adduction machine and spread your legs placing your knees and ankles behind the pads. Grasp the handles at your sides for support.

1. Slowly squeeze your legs together until your feet touch in front of you; 2. Slowly return your legs to the starting position without allowing the weight plates to touch; 3. Repeat as required.

Important: Leg adductions can be performed lying on your side using ankle or foot weights, using a low pulley while standing, or on a specialized leg adduction machine. Your range of motion using ankle or foot weights or with the low pulley is limited, therefore, a leg adduction machine is preferred.

LEG CURL ✓

Muscles Involved: The biceps femoris, semitendinosus, and semimembranosus (collectively, the hamstrings).

Execution: Position yourself on your stomach with your legs fully extended and knees slightly over the end of the pad. Place your heels under the roller pads and grasp the handles alongside the machine to stabilize your upper body.

1. Keep your hips on the bench and slowly curl your heels to your buttocks; 2. Slowly lower your heels back to the legs extended position; 3. Repeat as required.

Important: You can vary the muscles worked by pointing your toes straight or drawing them toward your shins. Pointing your toes will cause the hamstrings to do all the work. When drawn toward your shins, the calf muscles become involved as secondary movers. This method will provide additional calf development.

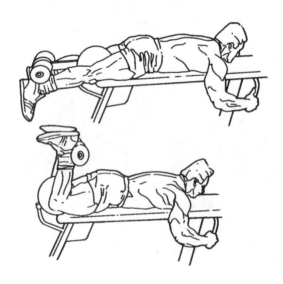

LEG EXTENSION ✓

Muscles Involved: The vastus lateralis, vastus medialis, vastus intermedius and rectus femoris (collectively, the quadriceps femoris muscle group).

Execution: Sit on the leg extension machine so your knees are comfortably at the end of the seat. Place your ankles behind and against the bottom rollers. If the machine has handles on the sides, grasp them. If it does not have handles, then lean back and support yourself holding onto the sides of the bench.

1. Slowly push up against the bottom roller with your feet so your legs and knee joints are completely extended; 2. Slowly allow your legs to return to the starting position without allowing the weight plates to touch; 3. Repeat as required.

Important: It is important to lock your knees out for maximum muscle contraction. You also have the option of performing single leg extensions by selecting a lighter weight and alternating legs.

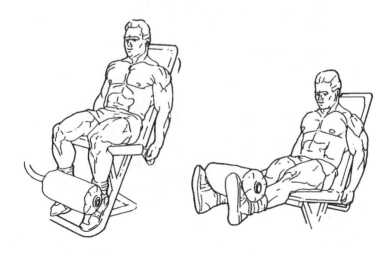

LEG PRESS

Muscles Involved: Biceps femoris, semitendinosus, and semi-membranosus (collectively, the hamstrings); vastus lateralis, vastus medialis, vastus intermedius and rectus femoris (collectively, the quadriceps femoris muscle group), and gluteus maximus.

Execution: Adjust the angled back pad and sit into the leg press placing your feet on the pushing plate. Press the plate up and release the restraining handles.

1. Bend your knees and slowly lower the weight plate bringing your legs to a 90-degree angle; 2. Slowly press the weight plate back up until your legs are fully extended (do not lock your knees); 3. Repeat as required.

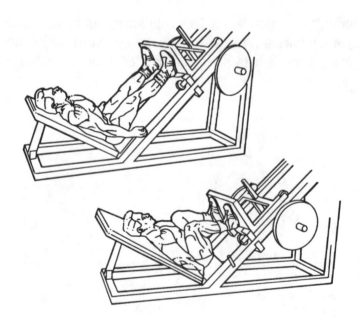

LUNGE ✓

Muscles Involved: The vastus lateralis, vastus medialis, vastus intermedius and rectus femoris (collectively, the quadriceps femoris muscle group); biceps femoris, semitendinosus, semimembranosus (collectively, the hamstrings), gluteus maximus, and spinalis.

Execution: Assume a standing position with your feet slightly less than shoulder-width apart. Grasp a barbell with a wider than shoulder-width grip and place it across your chest (beginners) or shoulders (intermediate/advanced).

1. Keeping your back vertical and slightly arched, slowly step forward with one leg making a long stride, lowering the body down and forward until the rear knee lightly touches the floor; 2. Shift your weight backward by taking several short steps rearward to return to the starting position; 3. Step out with the other leg; 4. Repeat as required alternating legs.

Important: It is recommended that beginners perform the lunge with the wooden stick or unloaded barbell across the upper chest. This will force you to keep your trunk erect as you learn the movement, preventing possible injury.

SQUAT

Muscles Involved: The vastus lateralis, vastus medialis, vastus intermedius and rectus femoris (collectively, the quadriceps femoris muscle group); biceps femoris, semitendinosus, and semimembranosus (collectively, the upper hamstrings), iliocostalis thoracis, iliocostalis lumborum, longissimus dorsi and spinalis dorsi (collectively, the erector spinae muscle group), and gluteus maximus.

Execution: Step into the squat rack and place the barbell across the shoulders and resting on the upper trapezius. Grip the bar wider than your shoulders using the bar marks for equal distance. Stand with your feet shoulder-width apart, toes pointed slightly outward. Distribute your body weight equally between both feet.

1. Keeping the heels in contact with the floor at all times, slowly lower into the squat position. (The knees will move slightly forward, the buttocks will move slightly to the rear and then straight down, and the trunk should incline forward slightly); 2. Slowly straighten your legs keeping your head and chest up during the upward drive; 3. Repeat as required.

10
CALF
EXERCISES

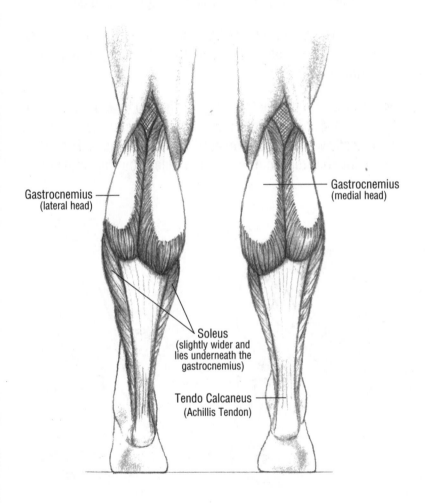

Gastrocnemius
(lateral head)

Gastrocnemius
(medial head)

Soleus
(slightly wider and
lies underneath the
gastrocnemius)

Tendo Calcaneus
(Achillis Tendon)

DONKEY CALF RAISE

Muscles Involved: The gatrocnemius and soleus.

Execution: Stand on the edge of a 2-4 inch platform with your heels extended over the edge. Bend over 90 degrees at the waist, supporting your upper body with a piece of exercise equipment. Have your training partner sit on your hips as far back as possible, keeping your legs straight and knees locked.

1. Slowly rise up on the balls of your feet as far as possible; 2. Slowly return to the starting position; 3. Repeat as required.

Important: To increase the range of motion, stand on a wooden block 1-4 inches high. Changing the position of your feet periodically will help develop assisting calf muscles. For example, point your toes in or out and/or place your feet at different widths.

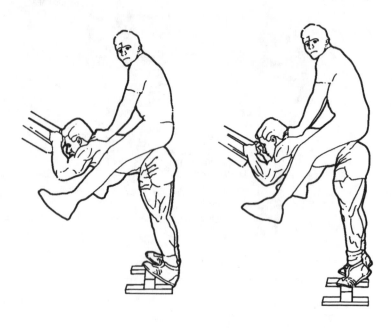

SEATED CALF RAISE

Muscles Involved: The soleus.

Execution: Sit on the calf machine placing the balls of your feet on the floor bar. Your heels should be free to rise up and down. Adjust the resistance pads so they rest on your lower thighs.

1. Slowly raise your heels up as high as possible; 2. Slowly lower your heels until they are fully stretched; 3. Rise your heels again and repeat as required.

Important: For greater calf development, hold your position on the top of the movement for 5-6 seconds. The soleus muscle has two heads. Pointing the toes in will develop the medial head. Pointing the toes out will develop the lateral head, which is used mainly for stability.

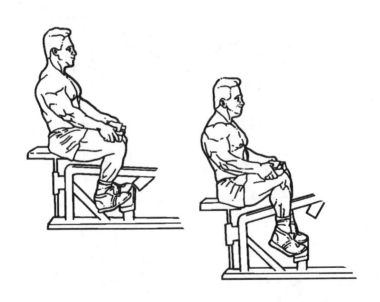

STANDING CALF RAISE

Muscles Involved: The gatrocnemius and soleus.

Execution: Step into a standing calf raise machine and place your shoulders under the pads. Bend your knees, positioning your toes on the block with your heels extended off the edge. Grasp the machine for support.

1. Slowly straighten your legs, keeping the knees slightly bent, then raise up on your toes as far as possible;
2. Slowly lower your heels toward the floor as far as possible; 3. Repeat as required.

Important: To develop assisting muscles, change your foot position. For example, point the toes inward or outward and place the feet wider or narrower.

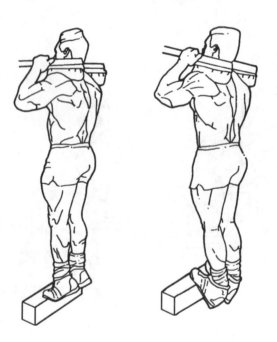

11
WEIGHT
TRAINING
RECORDS

Short-Term
Fitness Goals

Progress Graphs

Date _____   **Weight** _____   **Time** _____

Exercises	1 Rep	Wt	2 Rep	Wt	3 Rep	Wt	4 Rep	Wt	5 Rep	Wt	6 Rep	Wt

Notes:

Daily Calorie Intake: _____   Protein Intake: _____   Carb. Intake: _____   Fat Intake: _____

Date _____ **Weight** _____ **Time** _____

Exercises	1		2		3		4		5		6	
	Rep	Wt	Rep	Wt	Rep	Wt	Rep	Wt	Rep	Wt	Rep	Wt

Notes:

Daily Calorie Intake: _____ **Protein Intake:** _____ **Carb. Intake:** _____ **Fat Intake:** _____

Date _____ **Weight** _____ **Time** _____

Exercises	1 Rep	Wt	2 Rep	Wt	3 Rep	Wt	4 Rep	Wt	5 Rep	Wt	6 Rep	Wt

Notes:

Daily Calorie Intake: _____ Protein Intake: _____ Carb. Intake: _____ Fat Intake: _____

Date _____ **Weight** _____ **Time** _____

Exercises	1 Rep	Wt	2 Rep	Wt	3 Rep	Wt	4 Rep	Wt	5 Rep	Wt	6 Rep	Wt

Notes: _____

Daily Calorie Intake: _____ **Protein Intake:** _____ **Carb. Intake:** _____ **Fat Intake:** _____

Date _____ Weight _____ Time _____

Exercises

Exercises	1 Rep	Wt	2 Rep	Wt	3 Rep	Wt	4 Rep	Wt	5 Rep	Wt	6 Rep	Wt

Notes:

Daily Calorie Intake: _____ Protein Intake: _____ Carb. Intake: _____ Fat Intake: _____

Exercises

Date _____ Weight _____ Time _____

Exercises	1 Rep	Wt	2 Rep	Wt	3 Rep	Wt	4 Rep	Wt	5 Rep	Wt	6 Rep	Wt

Notes: _____

Daily Calorie Intake: _____ **Protein Intake:** _____ **Carb. Intake:** _____ **Fat Intake:** _____

Date _____ **Weight** _____ **Time** _____

Exercises	1 Rep	Wt	2 Rep	Wt	3 Rep	Wt	4 Rep	Wt	5 Rep	Wt	6 Rep	Wt

Notes:

Daily Calorie Intake: _____ Protein Intake: _____ Carb. Intake: _____ Fat Intake: _____

Date _____ **Weight** _____ **Time** _____

Exercises	1 Rep	Wt	2 Rep	Wt	3 Rep	Wt	4 Rep	Wt	5 Rep	Wt	6 Rep	Wt

Notes: _____

Daily Calorie Intake: _____ **Protein Intake:** _____ **Carb. Intake:** _____ **Fat Intake:** _____

Exercises

Date _____ **Weight** _____ **Time** _____

	1		2		3		4		5		6	
	Rep	Wt	Rep	Wt	Rep	Wt	Rep	Wt	Rep	Wt	Rep	Wt

Notes:

Daily Calorie Intake: _____ **Protein Intake:** _____ **Carb. Intake:** _____ **Fat Intake:** _____

Exercises

	1		2		3		4		5		6	
	Rep	Wt	Rep	Wt	Rep	Wt	Rep	Wt	Rep	Wt	Rep	Wt

Date _____ **Weight** _____ **Time** _____

Notes:

Daily Calorie Intake: _____ **Protein Intake:** _____ **Carb. Intake:** _____ **Fat Intake:** _____

Exercises

Date _____					Weight _____					Time _____			
	1		2		3		4		5		6	
	Rep	Wt	Rep	Wt	Rep	Wt	Rep	Wt	Rep	Wt	Rep	Wt

Notes:

Daily Calorie Intake: _____ Protein Intake: _____ Carb. Intake: _____ Fat Intake: _____

Date _____ Weight _____ Time

Exercises

	1 Rep	Wt	2 Rep	Wt	3 Rep	Wt	4 Rep	Wt	5 Rep	Wt	6 Rep	Wt

Notes: _____

Daily Calorie Intake: _____ Protein Intake: _____ Carb. Intake: _____ Fat Intake: _____

Exercises

Date _____ Weight _____ Time _____

Exercises	1 Rep	Wt	2 Rep	Wt	3 Rep	Wt	4 Rep	Wt	5 Rep	Wt	6 Rep	Wt

Notes:

Daily Calorie Intake: _____   Protein Intake: _____   Carb. Intake: _____   Fat Intake: _____

Exercises

Date _____ **Weight** _____ **Time** _____

Exercises	1		2		3		4		5		6	
	Rep	Wt	Rep	Wt	Rep	Wt	Rep	Wt	Rep	Wt	Rep	Wt

Notes:

Daily Calorie Intake: _____ **Protein Intake:** _____ **Carb. Intake:** _____ **Fat Intake:** _____

Date _____ **Weight** _____ **Time** _____

Exercises	1 Rep	Wt	2 Rep	Wt	3 Rep	Wt	4 Rep	Wt	5 Rep	Wt	6 Rep	Wt

Notes:

Daily Calorie Intake: _____ **Protein Intake:** _____ **Carb. Intake:** _____ **Fat Intake:** _____

Exercises

Date _____ **Weight** _____ **Time** _____

Exercises	1 Rep	Wt	2 Rep	Wt	3 Rep	Wt	4 Rep	Wt	5 Rep	Wt	6 Rep	Wt

Notes: _____

Daily Calorie Intake: _____ **Protein Intake:** _____ **Carb. Intake:** _____ **Fat Intake:** _____

Exercises

Exercises	Date ___						Weight ___						Time ___					
	1	Rep	Wt	2	Rep	Wt	3	Rep	Wt	4	Rep	Wt	5	Rep	Wt	6	Rep	Wt

Notes:

Daily Calorie Intake: _____ **Protein Intake:** _____ **Carb. Intake:** _____ **Fat Intake:** _____

Exercises

		1	Rep	Wt	2	Rep	Wt	3	Rep	Wt	4	Rep	Wt	5	Rep	Wt	6	Rep	Wt

Date _____ **Weight** _____ **Time** _____

Notes:
_____

Daily Calorie Intake: _____ **Protein Intake:** _____ **Carb. Intake:** _____ **Fat Intake:** _____

Date _____ **Weight** _____ **Time** _____

Exercises	1 Rep	Wt	2 Rep	Wt	3 Rep	Wt	4 Rep	Wt	5 Rep	Wt	6 Rep	Wt

Notes:

Daily Calorie Intake: _____ **Protein Intake:** _____ **Carb. Intake:** _____ **Fat Intake:** _____

Date _____ **Weight** _____ **Time** _____

Exercises

Exercises	1 Rep	Wt	2 Rep	Wt	3 Rep	Wt	4 Rep	Wt	5 Rep	Wt	6 Rep	Wt

Notes: _____

Daily Calorie Intake: _____   **Protein Intake:** _____   **Carb. Intake:** _____   **Fat Intake:** _____

Date _____ **Weight** _____ **Time** _____

Exercises	1 Rep	Wt	2 Rep	Wt	3 Rep	Wt	4 Rep	Wt	5 Rep	Wt	6 Rep	Wt

Notes:

Daily Calorie Intake: _____ **Protein Intake:** _____ **Carb. Intake:** _____ **Fat Intake:** _____

Exercises

Date _____ **Weight** _____ **Time** _____

Exercises	1 Rep	Wt	2 Rep	Wt	3 Rep	Wt	4 Rep	Wt	5 Rep	Wt	6 Rep	Wt

Notes: _____

Daily Calorie Intake: _____ **Protein Intake:** _____ **Carb. Intake:** _____ **Fat Intake:** _____

Date _____ **Weight** _____ **Time** _____

Exercises	1 Rep	Wt	2 Rep	Wt	3 Rep	Wt	4 Rep	Wt	5 Rep	Wt	6 Rep	Wt

Notes: _____

Daily Calorie Intake: _____ **Protein Intake:** _____ **Carb. Intake:** _____ **Fat Intake:** _____

Exercises

	1		2		3		4		5		6	
	Rep	Wt	Rep	Wt	Rep	Wt	Rep	Wt	Rep	Wt	Rep	Wt

Date _____ **Weight** _____ **Time** _____

Notes:

Daily Calorie Intake: _____ **Protein Intake:** _____ **Carb. Intake:** _____ **Fat Intake:** _____

Exercises

	Date		Weight		Time	
	1 Rep	Wt	2 Rep	Wt	3 Rep	Wt	4 Rep	Wt	5 Rep	Wt	6 Rep	Wt

Notes:

Daily Calorie Intake: _____ Protein Intake: _____ Carb. Intake: _____ Fat Intake: _____

Date _____ **Weight** _____ **Time** _____

Exercises	1		2		3		4		5		6	
	Rep	Wt	Rep	Wt	Rep	Wt	Rep	Wt	Rep	Wt	Rep	Wt

Notes: _____

Daily Calorie Intake: _____ Protein Intake: _____ Carb. Intake: _____ Fat Intake: _____

Exercises

Date _____ **Weight** _____ **Time** _____

Exercises	1 Rep	Wt	2 Rep	Wt	3 Rep	Wt	4 Rep	Wt	5 Rep	Wt	6 Rep	Wt

Notes:

Daily Calorie Intake: _____ Protein Intake: _____ Carb. Intake: _____ Fat Intake: _____

Exercises

	1	Rep	Wt	2	Rep	Wt	3	Rep	Wt	4	Rep	Wt	5	Rep	Wt	6	Rep	Wt

Date _____ **Weight** _____ **Time** _____

Notes:

Daily Calorie Intake: _____ **Protein Intake:** _____ **Carb. Intake:** _____ **Fat Intake:** _____

Date _____ **Weight** _____ **Time** _____

Exercises	1 Rep	Wt	2 Rep	Wt	3 Rep	Wt	4 Rep	Wt	5 Rep	Wt	6 Rep	Wt

Notes: _____

Daily Calorie Intake: _____ Protein Intake: _____ Carb. Intake: _____ Fat Intake: _____

Date _____									Weight _____								Time _____		

Exercises

	1 Rep	Wt	2 Rep	Wt	3 Rep	Wt	4 Rep	Wt	5 Rep	Wt	6 Rep	Wt

Notes: _____

Daily Calorie Intake: _____   Protein Intake: _____   Carb. Intake: _____   Fat Intake: _____

Exercises

Date _____ Weight _____ Time _____

Exercises	1 Rep	Wt	2 Rep	Wt	3 Rep	Wt	4 Rep	Wt	5 Rep	Wt	6 Rep	Wt

Notes: _____

Daily Calorie Intake: _____ Protein Intake: _____ Carb. Intake: _____ Fat Intake: _____

Date _____ **Weight** _____ **Time** _____

Exercises

	1		2		3		4		5		6	
	Rep	Wt	Rep	Wt	Rep	Wt	Rep	Wt	Rep	Wt	Rep	Wt

Notes: _____

Daily Calorie Intake: _____ **Protein Intake:** _____ **Carb. Intake:** _____ **Fat Intake:** _____

Date _____ **Weight** _____ **Time** _____

Exercises	1 Rep	Wt	2 Rep	Wt	3 Rep	Wt	4 Rep	Wt	5 Rep	Wt	6 Rep	Wt

Notes:

Daily Calorie Intake: _____   Protein Intake: _____   Carb. Intake: _____   Fat Intake: _____

Exercises

Date _____ **Weight** _____ **Time** _____

	1		2		3		4		5		6	
	Rep	Wt	Rep	Wt	Rep	Wt	Rep	Wt	Rep	Wt	Rep	Wt

Notes:

Daily Calorie Intake: _____ **Protein Intake:** _____ **Carb. Intake:** _____ **Fat Intake:** _____

Exercises

Date _____ Weight _____ Time _____

	1 Rep	Wt	2 Rep	Wt	3 Rep	Wt	4 Rep	Wt	5 Rep	Wt	6 Rep	Wt

Notes:

Daily Calorie Intake: _____ Protein Intake: _____ Carb. Intake: _____ Fat Intake: _____

Exercises

Date _____ **Weight** _____ **Time** _____

	1	Rep	Wt	2	Rep	Wt	3	Rep	Wt	4	Rep	Wt	5	Rep	Wt	6	Rep	Wt

Notes:

Daily Calorie Intake: _____ **Protein Intake:** _____ **Carb. Intake:** _____ **Fat Intake:** _____

Date _____ **Weight** _____ **Time** _____

Exercises	1 Rep	Wt	2 Rep	Wt	3 Rep	Wt	4 Rep	Wt	5 Rep	Wt	6 Rep	Wt

Notes:

Daily Calorie Intake: _____ **Protein Intake:** _____ **Carb. Intake:** _____ **Fat Intake:** _____

Date _____ **Weight** _____ **Time** _____

Exercises	1 Rep	Wt	2 Rep	Wt	3 Rep	Wt	4 Rep	Wt	5 Rep	Wt	6 Rep	Wt

Notes: _____

Daily Calorie Intake: _____ Protein Intake: _____ Carb. Intake: _____ Fat Intake: _____

Exercises

Date					Weight							Time			
1 Rep	Wt	2 Rep	Wt	3 Rep	Wt	4 Rep	Wt	5 Rep	Wt	6 Rep	Wt				

Notes:

Daily Calorie Intake: **Protein Intake:**   **Carb. Intake:**   **Fat Intake:**

Exercises	1 Rep	Wt	2 Rep	Wt	3 Rep	Wt	4 Rep	Wt	5 Rep	Wt	6 Rep	Wt

Date _____ **Weight** _____ **Time** _____

Notes:

Daily Calorie Intake: _____   Protein Intake: _____   Carb. Intake: _____   Fat Intake: _____

Date _____ **Weight** _____ **Time** _____

Exercises	1 Rep	Wt	2 Rep	Wt	3 Rep	Wt	4 Rep	Wt	5 Rep	Wt	6 Rep	Wt

Notes:

Daily Calorie Intake: _____ Protein Intake: _____ Carb. Intake: _____ Fat Intake: _____

Exercises

Date _____ **Weight** _____ **Time** _____

	1		2		3		4		5		6	
	Rep	Wt	Rep	Wt	Rep	Wt	Rep	Wt	Rep	Wt	Rep	Wt

Notes:

Daily Calorie Intake: _____ **Protein Intake:** _____ **Carb. Intake:** _____ **Fat Intake:** _____

Date _____ **Weight** _____ **Time** _____

Exercises	1 Rep	Wt	2 Rep	Wt	3 Rep	Wt	4 Rep	Wt	5 Rep	Wt	6 Rep	Wt

Notes:

Daily Calorie Intake: _____ **Protein Intake:** _____ **Carb. Intake:** _____ **Fat Intake:** _____

Date _____ **Weight** _____ **Time** _____

Exercises

	1		2		3		4		5		6	
	Rep	Wt	Rep	Wt	Rep	Wt	Rep	Wt	Rep	Wt	Rep	Wt

Notes: _____

Daily Calorie Intake: _____ **Protein Intake:** _____ **Carb. Intake:** _____ **Fat Intake:** _____

Exercises

	Date _____					Weight _____					Time _____			
	1		2		3		4		5		6	
	Rep	Wt	Rep	Wt	Rep	Wt	Rep	Wt	Rep	Wt	Rep	Wt

Notes:

Daily Calorie Intake: _____ Protein Intake: _____ Carb. Intake: _____ Fat Intake: _____

Date _____ Weight _____ Time _____

Exercises	1 Rep	Wt	2 Rep	Wt	3 Rep	Wt	4 Rep	Wt	5 Rep	Wt	6 Rep	Wt

Notes:

Daily Calorie Intake: _____   Protein Intake: _____   Carb. Intake: _____   Fat Intake: _____

Exercises

Date _____ Weight _____ Time _____

	1		2		3		4		5		6	
	Rep	Wt	Rep	Wt	Rep	Wt	Rep	Wt	Rep	Wt	Rep	Wt

Notes: _____

Daily Calorie Intake: _____ Protein Intake: _____ Carb. Intake: _____ Fat Intake: _____

Date _____ **Weight** _____ **Time** _____

Exercises	1 Rep	Wt	2 Rep	Wt	3 Rep	Wt	4 Rep	Wt	5 Rep	Wt	6 Rep	Wt

Notes:

Daily Calorie Intake: _____ **Protein Intake:** _____ **Carb. Intake:** _____ **Fat Intake:** _____

Exercises

Date _____ **Weight** _____ **Time** _____

Exercises	1		2		3		4		5		6	
	Rep	Wt	Rep	Wt	Rep	Wt	Rep	Wt	Rep	Wt	Rep	Wt

Notes: _____

Daily Calorie Intake: _____ Protein Intake: _____ Carb. Intake: _____ Fat Intake: _____

Exercises

Date _____ **Weight** _____ **Time** _____

Exercises	1		2		3		4		5		6	
	Rep	Wt	Rep	Wt	Rep	Wt	Rep	Wt	Rep	Wt	Rep	Wt

Notes: _____

Daily Calorie Intake: _____ Protein Intake: _____ Carb. Intake: _____ Fat Intake: _____

Exercises

Date _____ **Weight** _____ **Time** _____

Exercises	1		2		3		4		5		6	
	Rep	Wt	Rep	Wt	Rep	Wt	Rep	Wt	Rep	Wt	Rep	Wt

Notes:

Daily Calorie Intake: _____ Protein Intake: _____ Carb. Intake: _____ Fat Intake: _____

Date _____ Weight _____ Time _____

Exercises	1 Rep	Wt	2 Rep	Wt	3 Rep	Wt	4 Rep	Wt	5 Rep	Wt	6 Rep	Wt

Notes: _____

Daily Calorie Intake: _____   Protein Intake: _____   Carb. Intake: _____   Fat Intake: _____

Exercises | **Date** _____ | **Weight** _____ | **Time** _____

Exercises	1	Rep	Wt	2	Rep	Wt	3	Rep	Wt	4	Rep	Wt	5	Rep	Wt	6	Rep	Wt

Notes:

Daily Calorie Intake: _____ **Protein Intake:** _____ **Carb. Intake:** _____ **Fat Intake:** _____

Date _____ **Weight** _____ **Time** _____

Exercises	1 Rep	Wt	2 Rep	Wt	3 Rep	Wt	4 Rep	Wt	5 Rep	Wt	6 Rep	Wt

Notes:

Daily Calorie Intake: **Protein Intake:**   **Carb. Intake:**   **Fat Intake:**

Exercises

Exercises	Date _____						Weight _____						Time _____					
	1		2		3		4		5		6	
	Rep	Wt	Rep	Wt	Rep	Wt	Rep	Wt	Rep	Wt	Rep	Wt

Notes: _____

Daily Calorie Intake: _____   Protein Intake: _____   Carb. Intake: _____   Fat Intake: _____

Date _____ **Weight** _____ **Time** _____

Exercises	1		2		3		4		5		6	
	Rep	Wt	Rep	Wt	Rep	Wt	Rep	Wt	Rep	Wt	Rep	Wt

Notes:

Daily Calorie Intake: _____ Protein Intake: _____ Carb. Intake: _____ Fat Intake: _____

Exercises

Date _____ Weight _____ Time _____

	1		2		3		4		5		6	
	Rep	Wt	Rep	Wt	Rep	Wt	Rep	Wt	Rep	Wt	Rep	Wt

Notes: _____

Daily Calorie Intake: _____ Protein Intake: _____ Carb. Intake: _____ Fat Intake: _____

Date _____ **Weight** _____ **Time** _____

Exercises

	1		2		3		4		5		6	
	Rep	Wt	Rep	Wt	Rep	Wt	Rep	Wt	Rep	Wt	Rep	Wt

Notes: _____

Daily Calorie Intake: _____ **Protein Intake:** _____ **Carb. Intake:** _____ **Fat Intake:** _____

Date _____ Weight _____ Time _____

Exercises	1 Rep	Wt	2 Rep	Wt	3 Rep	Wt	4 Rep	Wt	5 Rep	Wt	6 Rep	Wt

Notes:

Daily Calorie Intake: _____   Protein Intake: _____   Carb. Intake: _____   Fat Intake: _____

Exercises

Date _____ Weight _____ Time _____

	1		2		3		4		5		6	
	Rep	Wt	Rep	Wt	Rep	Wt	Rep	Wt	Rep	Wt	Rep	Wt

Notes: _____

Daily Calorie Intake: _____   **Protein Intake:** _____   **Carb. Intake:** _____   **Fat Intake:** _____

Date _____ **Weight** _____ **Time** _____

Exercises	1 Rep	Wt	2 Rep	Wt	3 Rep	Wt	4 Rep	Wt	5 Rep	Wt	6 Rep	Wt

Notes: _____

Daily Calorie Intake: _____ **Protein Intake:** _____ **Carb. Intake:** _____ **Fat Intake:** _____

Date _____ **Weight** _____ **Time** _____

Exercises	1 Rep	Wt	2 Rep	Wt	3 Rep	Wt	4 Rep	Wt	5 Rep	Wt	6 Rep	Wt

Notes:

Daily Calorie Intake: _____ **Protein Intake:** _____ **Carb. Intake:** _____ **Fat Intake:** _____

Date _____ **Weight** _____ **Time** _____

Exercises	1 Rep	Wt	2 Rep	Wt	3 Rep	Wt	4 Rep	Wt	5 Rep	Wt	6 Rep	Wt

Notes:

Daily Calorie Intake: _____ Protein Intake: _____ Carb. Intake: _____ Fat Intake: _____

Date _____ **Weight** _____ **Time** _____

Exercises	1 Rep	Wt	2 Rep	Wt	3 Rep	Wt	4 Rep	Wt	5 Rep	Wt	6 Rep	Wt

Notes:

Daily Calorie Intake: _____ **Protein Intake:** _____ **Carb. Intake:** _____ **Fat Intake:** _____

Exercises

Date _____ Weight _____ Time _____

Exercises	1 Rep	Wt	2 Rep	Wt	3 Rep	Wt	4 Rep	Wt	5 Rep	Wt	6 Rep	Wt

Notes: _____

Daily Calorie Intake: _____ Protein Intake: _____ Carb. Intake: _____ Fat Intake: _____

Date _____ **Weight** _____ **Time** _____

Exercises

Exercises	1 Rep	Wt	2 Rep	Wt	3 Rep	Wt	4 Rep	Wt	5 Rep	Wt	6 Rep	Wt

Notes:

Daily Calorie Intake: _____ **Protein Intake:** _____ **Carb. Intake:** _____ **Fat Intake:** _____

Exercises

Date _____ **Weight** _____ **Time** _____

	1		2		3		4		5		6	
	Rep	Wt	Rep	Wt	Rep	Wt	Rep	Wt	Rep	Wt	Rep	Wt

Notes: _____

Daily Calorie Intake: _____   Protein Intake: _____   Carb. Intake: _____   Fat Intake: _____

Date _____ **Weight** _____ **Time** _____

Exercises	1 Rep	Wt	2 Rep	Wt	3 Rep	Wt	4 Rep	Wt	5 Rep	Wt	6 Rep	Wt

Notes: _____

Daily Calorie Intake: _____ **Protein Intake:** _____ **Carb. Intake:** _____ **Fat Intake:** _____

Date _____ **Weight** _____ **Time** _____

Exercises	1		2		3		4		5		6	
	Rep	Wt	Rep	Wt	Rep	Wt	Rep	Wt	Rep	Wt	Rep	Wt

Notes:

Daily Calorie Intake: _____ **Protein Intake:** _____ **Carb. Intake:** _____ **Fat Intake:** _____

Exercises

	Date				Weight					Time			
	1 Rep	Wt	**2** Rep	Wt	**3** Rep	Wt	**4** Rep	Wt	**5** Rep	Wt	**6** Rep	Wt	

Notes:

Daily Calorie Intake: _____   Protein Intake: _____   Carb. Intake: _____   Fat Intake: _____

Exercises

Date _____ Weight _____ Time _____

Exercises	1 Rep	Wt	2 Rep	Wt	3 Rep	Wt	4 Rep	Wt	5 Rep	Wt	6 Rep	Wt

Notes: _____

Daily Calorie Intake: _____ Protein Intake: _____ Carb. Intake: _____ Fat Intake: _____

Date _____ **Weight** _____ **Time** _____

Exercises	1 Rep	Wt	2 Rep	Wt	3 Rep	Wt	4 Rep	Wt	5 Rep	Wt	6 Rep	Wt

Notes:

Daily Calorie Intake: _____ **Protein Intake:** _____ **Carb. Intake:** _____ **Fat Intake:** _____

Date _____   Weight _____   Time _____

Exercises	1 Rep	Wt	2 Rep	Wt	3 Rep	Wt	4 Rep	Wt	5 Rep	Wt	6 Rep	Wt

Notes:

Daily Calorie Intake: _____   Protein Intake: _____   Carb. Intake: _____   Fat Intake: _____

Date _____ **Weight** _____ **Time** _____

Exercises	1 Rep	Wt	2 Rep	Wt	3 Rep	Wt	4 Rep	Wt	5 Rep	Wt	6 Rep	Wt

Notes: _____

Daily Calorie Intake: _____ **Protein Intake:** _____ **Carb. Intake:** _____ **Fat Intake:** _____

Exercises | **Date** _____ **Weight** _____ **Time** _____

Exercises	1 Rep	Wt	2 Rep	Wt	3 Rep	Wt	4 Rep	Wt	5 Rep	Wt	6 Rep	Wt

Notes: _____

Daily Calorie Intake: _____   **Protein Intake:** _____   **Carb. Intake:** _____   **Fat Intake:** _____

Date _____ **Weight** _____ **Time** _____

Exercises	1 Rep	Wt	2 Rep	Wt	3 Rep	Wt	4 Rep	Wt	5 Rep	Wt	6 Rep	Wt

Notes:

Daily Calorie Intake: _____   Protein Intake: _____   Carb. Intake: _____   Fat Intake: _____

Exercises

| Date | Weight | Time |

Exercises

	1		2		3		4		5		6	
	Rep	Wt	Rep	Wt	Rep	Wt	Rep	Wt	Rep	Wt	Rep	Wt

Notes:

Daily Calorie Intake: Protein Intake: Carb. Intake: Fat Intake:

Date _____ **Weight** _____ **Time** _____

Exercises

	1		2		3		4		5		6	
	Rep	Wt	Rep	Wt	Rep	Wt	Rep	Wt	Rep	Wt	Rep	Wt

Notes:

Daily Calorie Intake: _____   **Protein Intake:** _____   **Carb. Intake:** _____   **Fat Intake:** _____

Exercises

Date _____ **Weight** _____ **Time** _____

Exercises	1 Rep	Wt	2 Rep	Wt	3 Rep	Wt	4 Rep	Wt	5 Rep	Wt	6 Rep	Wt

Notes:

Daily Calorie Intake: _____ Protein Intake: _____ Carb. Intake: _____ Fat Intake: _____

Exercises

	1 Rep	Wt	2 Rep	Wt	3 Rep	Wt	4 Rep	Wt	5 Rep	Wt	6 Rep	Wt

Date _____ Weight _____ Time

Notes:

Daily Calorie Intake: _____ **Protein Intake:** _____ **Carb. Intake:** _____ **Fat Intake:** _____

Exercises

Date _____ **Weight** _____ **Time** _____

Exercises	1 Rep	Wt	2 Rep	Wt	3 Rep	Wt	4 Rep	Wt	5 Rep	Wt	6 Rep	Wt

Notes:

Daily Calorie Intake: _____ Protein Intake: _____ Carb. Intake: _____ Fat Intake: _____

Date _____ **Weight** _____ **Time** _____

Exercises	1		2		3		4		5		6	
	Rep	Wt	Rep	Wt	Rep	Wt	Rep	Wt	Rep	Wt	Rep	Wt

Notes:

Daily Calorie Intake: _____ Protein Intake: _____ Carb. Intake: _____ Fat Intake: _____

Date _____ **Weight** _____ **Time** _____

Exercises	1 Rep	Wt	2 Rep	Wt	3 Rep	Wt	4 Rep	Wt	5 Rep	Wt	6 Rep	Wt

Notes:

Daily Calorie Intake: _____ Protein Intake: _____ Carb. Intake: _____ Fat Intake: _____

Date _____ **Weight** _____ **Time** _____

Exercises	1 Rep	Wt	2 Rep	Wt	3 Rep	Wt	4 Rep	Wt	5 Rep	Wt	6 Rep	Wt

Notes:

Daily Calorie Intake: _____ Protein Intake: _____ Carb. Intake: _____ Fat Intake: _____

Exercises | Date _____ | Weight _____ | Time _____

Exercises	1 Rep	Wt	2 Rep	Wt	3 Rep	Wt	4 Rep	Wt	5 Rep	Wt	6 Rep	Wt

Notes:

Daily Calorie Intake: _____ Protein Intake: _____ Carb. Intake: _____ Fat Intake: _____

Exercises	1		2		3		4		5		6	
	Rep	Wt	Rep	Wt	Rep	Wt	Rep	Wt	Rep	Wt	Rep	Wt

Date _____ Weight _____ Time _____

Notes: _____

Daily Calorie Intake: _____ **Protein Intake:** _____ **Carb. Intake:** _____ **Fat Intake:** _____

Date _____ **Weight** _____ **Time** _____

Exercises	1 Rep	Wt	2 Rep	Wt	3 Rep	Wt	4 Rep	Wt	5 Rep	Wt	6 Rep	Wt

Notes: _____

Daily Calorie Intake: _____ Protein Intake: _____ Carb. Intake: _____ Fat Intake: _____

Date _____ **Weight** _____ **Time** _____

Exercises	1 Rep	Wt	2 Rep	Wt	3 Rep	Wt	4 Rep	Wt	5 Rep	Wt	6 Rep	Wt

Notes:

Daily Calorie Intake:	Protein Intake:	Carb. Intake:	Fat Intake:

Exercises

Date _____ Weight _____ Time _____

	1		2		3		4		5		6	
	Rep	Wt	Rep	Wt	Rep	Wt	Rep	Wt	Rep	Wt	Rep	Wt

Notes:

Daily Calorie Intake: ____   Protein Intake: ____   Carb. Intake: ____   Fat Intake: ____

Date _____ **Weight** _____ **Time** _____

Exercises	1		2		3		4		5		6	
	Rep	Wt	Rep	Wt	Rep	Wt	Rep	Wt	Rep	Wt	Rep	Wt

Notes: _____

Daily Calorie Intake: _____ **Protein Intake:** _____ **Carb. Intake:** _____ **Fat Intake:** _____

Date _____ Weight _____ Time _____

Exercises	1		2		3		4		5		6	
	Rep	Wt	Rep	Wt	Rep	Wt	Rep	Wt	Rep	Wt	Rep	Wt

Notes:

Daily Calorie Intake: _____   Protein Intake: _____   Carb. Intake: _____   Fat Intake: _____

Date _____ Weight _____ Time _____

Exercises

Exercises	1 Rep	Wt	2 Rep	Wt	3 Rep	Wt	4 Rep	Wt	5 Rep	Wt	6 Rep	Wt

Notes: _____

Daily Calorie Intake: _____   Protein Intake: _____   Carb. Intake: _____   Fat Intake: _____

Date _____ Weight _____ Time _____

Exercises	1		2		3		4		5		6	
	Rep	Wt	Rep	Wt	Rep	Wt	Rep	Wt	Rep	Wt	Rep	Wt

Notes:

Daily Calorie Intake: _____ Protein Intake: _____ Carb. Intake: _____ Fat Intake: _____

Date _____ **Weight** _____ **Time** _____

Exercises	1 Rep	Wt	2 Rep	Wt	3 Rep	Wt	4 Rep	Wt	5 Rep	Wt	6 Rep	Wt

Notes:

Daily Calorie Intake: _____ Protein Intake: _____ Carb. Intake: _____ Fat Intake: _____

Date _____ **Weight** _____ **Time** _____

Exercises

Exercises	1 Rep	Wt	2 Rep	Wt	3 Rep	Wt	4 Rep	Wt	5 Rep	Wt	6 Rep	Wt

Notes: _____

Daily Calorie Intake: _____ Protein Intake: _____ Carb. Intake: _____ Fat Intake: _____

Date _____ Weight _____ Time _____

Exercises	1		2		3		4		5		6	
	Rep	Wt	Rep	Wt	Rep	Wt	Rep	Wt	Rep	Wt	Rep	Wt

Notes: _____

Daily Calorie Intake: _____ Protein Intake: _____ Carb. Intake: _____ Fat Intake: _____

Date _____ **Weight** _____ **Time** _____

Exercises	1 Rep	Wt	2 Rep	Wt	3 Rep	Wt	4 Rep	Wt	5 Rep	Wt	6 Rep	Wt

Notes: _____

Daily Calorie Intake: _____ **Protein Intake:** _____ **Carb. Intake:** _____ **Fat Intake:** _____

Date _____ **Weight** _____ **Time** _____

Exercises	1 Rep	Wt	2 Rep	Wt	3 Rep	Wt	4 Rep	Wt	5 Rep	Wt	6 Rep	Wt

Notes: _____

Daily Calorie Intake: _____ Protein Intake: _____ Carb. Intake: _____ Fat Intake: _____

Exercises	Date			Weight						Time					
	1 Rep	Wt	2 Rep	Wt	3 Rep	Wt	4 Rep	Wt	5 Rep	Wt	6 Rep	Wt			

Notes:

Daily Calorie Intake: Protein Intake: Carb. Intake: Fat Intake:

Exercises

Date _____			Weight _____				Time _____		

Exercises	1 Rep	Wt	2 Rep	Wt	3 Rep	Wt	4 Rep	Wt	5 Rep	Wt	6 Rep	Wt

Notes: _____

Daily Calorie Intake: _____ **Protein Intake:** _____ **Carb. Intake:** _____ **Fat Intake:** _____

Exercises

	Date ___				Weight ___					Time ___		
	1 Rep	Wt	**2** Rep	Wt	**3** Rep	Wt	**4** Rep	Wt	**5** Rep	Wt	**6** Rep	Wt

Notes:

Daily Calorie Intake: **Protein Intake:**   **Carb. Intake:**   **Fat Intake:**

Exercises   Date _____   Weight _____   Time _____

Exercises	1 Rep	Wt	2 Rep	Wt	3 Rep	Wt	4 Rep	Wt	5 Rep	Wt	6 Rep	Wt

Notes:

Daily Calorie Intake: _____   Protein Intake: _____   Carb. Intake: _____   Fat Intake: _____

Date _____ **Weight** _____ **Time** _____

Exercises	1 Rep	Wt	2 Rep	Wt	3 Rep	Wt	4 Rep	Wt	5 Rep	Wt	6 Rep	Wt

Notes:

Daily Calorie Intake: _____ Protein Intake: _____ Carb. Intake: _____ Fat Intake: _____

Date _____ **Weight** _____ **Time** _____

Exercises

	1 Rep	Wt	2 Rep	Wt	3 Rep	Wt	4 Rep	Wt	5 Rep	Wt	6 Rep	Wt

Notes:

Daily Calorie Intake: _____   Protein Intake: _____   Carb. Intake: _____   Fat Intake: _____

| Exercises | Date _____ Weight _____ Time _____ |||||||||||||
	1 Rep	Wt	2 Rep	Wt	3 Rep	Wt	4 Rep	Wt	5 Rep	Wt	6 Rep	Wt

Notes:

Daily Calorie Intake: _____ Protein Intake: _____ Carb. Intake: _____ Fat Intake: _____

Date _____ **Weight** _____ **Time** _____

Exercises	1 Rep	Wt	2 Rep	Wt	3 Rep	Wt	4 Rep	Wt	5 Rep	Wt	6 Rep	Wt

Notes: _____

Daily Calorie Intake: _____ **Protein Intake:** _____ **Carb. Intake:** _____ **Fat Intake:** _____

Exercises   Date _____   Weight _____   Time _____

Exercises	1 Rep	Wt	2 Rep	Wt	3 Rep	Wt	4 Rep	Wt	5 Rep	Wt	6 Rep	Wt

Notes:

Daily Calorie Intake: _____   Protein Intake: _____   Carb. Intake: _____   Fat Intake: _____

Date _____ **Weight** _____ **Time** _____

Exercises	1		2		3		4		5		6	
	Rep	Wt	Rep	Wt	Rep	Wt	Rep	Wt	Rep	Wt	Rep	Wt

Notes: _____

Daily Calorie Intake: _____ **Protein Intake:** _____ **Carb. Intake:** _____ **Fat Intake:** _____

Exercises

Date _____ **Weight** _____ **Time** _____

	1		2		3		4		5		6	
	Rep	Wt	Rep	Wt	Rep	Wt	Rep	Wt	Rep	Wt	Rep	Wt

Notes:

Daily Calorie Intake: _____ Protein Intake: _____ Carb. Intake: _____ Fat Intake: _____

Exercises

Date _____ Weight _____ Time _____

Exercises	1		2		3		4		5		6	
	Rep	Wt	Rep	Wt	Rep	Wt	Rep	Wt	Rep	Wt	Rep	Wt

Notes:

Daily Calorie Intake: _____ Protein Intake: _____ Carb. Intake: _____ Fat Intake: _____

Exercises

Date _____ Weight _____ Time _____

	1		2		3		4		5		6	
	Rep	Wt	Rep	Wt	Rep	Wt	Rep	Wt	Rep	Wt	Rep	Wt

Notes:

Daily Calorie Intake: _____ Protein Intake: _____ Carb. Intake: _____ Fat Intake: _____

Date _____ **Weight** _____ **Time** _____

Exercises	1 Rep	Wt	2 Rep	Wt	3 Rep	Wt	4 Rep	Wt	5 Rep	Wt	6 Rep	Wt

Notes:

Daily Calorie Intake: _____ **Protein Intake:** _____ **Carb. Intake:** _____ **Fat Intake:** _____

Exercises

Date _____ **Weight** _____ **Time** _____

Exercises	1		2		3		4		5		6	
	Rep	Wt	Rep	Wt	Rep	Wt	Rep	Wt	Rep	Wt	Rep	Wt

Notes:

Daily Calorie Intake: _____ **Protein Intake:** _____ **Carb. Intake:** _____ **Fat Intake:** _____

Date _____ **Weight** _____ **Time** _____

Exercises

Exercises	1		2		3		4		5		6	
	Rep	Wt	Rep	Wt	Rep	Wt	Rep	Wt	Rep	Wt	Rep	Wt

Notes: _____

Daily Calorie Intake: _____ **Protein Intake:** _____ **Carb. Intake:** _____ **Fat Intake:** _____

Date _____ **Weight** _____ **Time** _____

Exercises	1		2		3		4		5		6	
	Rep	Wt	Rep	Wt	Rep	Wt	Rep	Wt	Rep	Wt	Rep	Wt

Notes:

Daily Calorie Intake: _____ Protein Intake: _____ Carb. Intake: _____ Fat Intake: _____

Qty.	Title	Price	Total
	The Weight Training Workbook, 2nd Edition/Jim Bennett	$12.95	$
	The Weight Training Record, 2nd Edition/Jim Bennett	$10.95	$
	Getting in Shape/Bill Pearl	$15.00	$
	Getting Stronger/Bill Pearl & Gary Moran	$19.00	$
	Nutrition Almanac/Nutrition Search	$15.95	$
	Kinesiology of Exercise/Dr. Yessis, Ph.D.	$17.95	$
	Secrets of Soviet Sports Fitness & Training/Dr. Yessis, Ph.D.	$12.95	$
	Body Shaping for Women/Dr. Yessis, Ph.D.	$16.95	$
	(Video) Exercise Mastery/Dr. Yessis, Ph.D.	$39.00	$
	(Video) Stretching/ Bob Anderson	$29.95	$
	(Video) Keys to Weight Training for Men & Women/Bill Pearl	$19.95	$
	Praise! Walk/Integrity Music (Each series contains 2 cassette tapes)		
	Beginner – Get Going & Taking Charge, Plus Free Hip Pack	$19.95	$
	Intermediate – Walk by Faith & Power Stride	$19.95	$
	Advanced – Walk This Way & Higher Power	$19.95	$

U.S. Funds Only. Add $2.50 postage & handling for the first item and $1.00 for each additional
item. Wisconsin residents add 5% sales tax. For Priority Mail include an additional $2.00.

JBBA Publishing

P.O. Box 842

Appleton, WI 54912

1-800-245-7897

Name _____

Address _____

City/State/Zip _____

Telephone _____

VISA/MasterCard _____ Exp. _____

Allow 3-5 weeks. Satisfaction guaranteed or return for full refund.

Qty.	Title	Price	Total
	The Weight Training Workbook, 2nd Edition/Jim Bennett	$12.95	$
	The Weight Training Record, 2nd Edition/Jim Bennett	$10.95	$
	Getting in Shape/Bill Pearl	$15.00	$
	Getting Stronger/Bill Pearl & Gary Moran	$19.00	$
	Nutrition Almanac/Nutrition Search	$15.95	$
	Kinesiology of Exercise/Dr. Yessis, Ph.D.	$17.95	$
	Secrets of Soviet Sports Fitness & Training/Dr. Yessis, Ph.D.	$12.95	$
	Body Shaping for Women/Dr. Yessis, Ph.D.	$16.95	$
	(Video) Exercise Mastery/Dr. Yessis, Ph.D.	$39.00	$
	(Video) Stretching/ Bob Anderson	$29.95	$
	(Video) Keys to Weight Training for Men & Women/Bill Pearl	$19.95	$
	Praise! Walk/Integrity Music (Each series contains 2 cassette tapes)		
	Beginner – Get Going & Taking Charge, Plus Free Hip Pack	$19.95	$
	Intermediate – Walk by Faith & Power Stride	$19.95	$
	Advanced – Walk This Way & Higher Power	$19.95	$

U.S. Funds Only. Add $2.50 postage & handling for the first item and $1.00 for each additional
item. Wisconsin residents add 5% sales tax. For Priority Mail include an additional $2.00.

JBBA Publishing

P.O. Box 842

Appleton, WI 54912

1-800-245-7897

Name _____

Address _____

City/State/Zip _____

Telephone _____

VISA/MasterCard _____ Exp. _____

Allow 3-5 weeks. Satisfaction guaranteed or return for full refund.

Qty.	Title	Price	Total
	The Weight Training Workbook, 2nd Edition/Jim Bennett	$12.95	$
	The Weight Training Record, 2nd Edition/Jim Bennett	$10.95	$
	Getting in Shape/Bill Pearl	$15.00	$
	Getting Stronger/Bill Pearl & Gary Moran	$19.00	$
	Nutrition Almanac/Nutrition Search	$15.95	$
	Kinesiology of Exercise/Dr. Yessis, Ph.D.	$17.95	$
	Secrets of Soviet Sports Fitness & Training/Dr. Yessis, Ph.D.	$12.95	$
	Body Shaping for Women/Dr. Yessis, Ph.D.	$16.95	$
	(Video) Exercise Mastery/Dr. Yessis, Ph.D.	$39.00	$
	(Video) Stretching/ Bob Anderson	$29.95	$
	(Video) Keys to Weight Training for Men & Women/Bill Pearl	$19.95	$
	Praise! Walk/Integrity Music (Each series contains 2 cassette tapes)		
	Beginner – Get Going & Taking Charge, Plus Free Hip Pack	$19.95	$
	Intermediate – Walk by Faith & Power Stride	$19.95	$
	Advanced – Walk This Way & Higher Power	$19.95	$

U.S. Funds Only. Add $2.50 postage & handling for the first item and $1.00 for each additional item. Wisconsin residents add 5% sales tax. For Priority Mail include an additional $2.00.

JBBA Publishing
P.O. Box 842
Appleton, WI 54912
1-800-245-7897

Name _____

Address _____

City/State/Zip _____

Telephone _____

VISA/MasterCard _____ Exp. _____

Allow 3-5 weeks. Satisfaction guaranteed or return for full refund.

Qty.	Title	Price	Total
	The Weight Training Workbook, 2nd Edition/Jim Bennett	$12.95	$
	The Weight Training Record, 2nd Edition/Jim Bennett	$10.95	$
	Getting in Shape/Bill Pearl	$15.00	$
	Getting Stronger/Bill Pearl & Gary Moran	$19.00	$
	Nutrition Almanac/Nutrition Search	$15.95	$
	Kinesiology of Exercise/Dr. Yessis, Ph.D.	$17.95	$
	Secrets of Soviet Sports Fitness & Training/Dr. Yessis, Ph.D.	$12.95	$
	Body Shaping for Women/Dr. Yessis, Ph.D.	$16.95	$
	(Video) Exercise Mastery/Dr. Yessis, Ph.D.	$39.00	$
	(Video) Stretching/ Bob Anderson	$29.95	$
	(Video) Keys to Weight Training for Men & Women/Bill Pearl	$19.95	$
	Praise! Walk/Integrity Music (Each series contains 2 cassette tapes)		
	Beginner – Get Going & Taking Charge, Plus Free Hip Pack	$19.95	$
	Intermediate – Walk by Faith & Power Stride	$19.95	$
	Advanced – Walk This Way & Higher Power	$19.95	$

U.S. Funds Only. Add $2.50 postage & handling for the first item and $1.00 for each additional item. Wisconsin residents add 5% sales tax. For Priority Mail include an additional $2.00.

JBBA Publishing
P.O. Box 842
Appleton, WI 54912
1-800-245-7897

Name _____

Address _____

City/State/Zip _____

Telephone _____

VISA/MasterCard _____ Exp. _____

Allow 3-5 weeks. Satisfaction guaranteed or return for full refund.

Qty.	Title	Price	Total
	The Weight Training Workbook, 2nd Edition/Jim Bennett	$12.95	$
	The Weight Training Record, 2nd Edition/Jim Bennett	$10.95	$
	Getting in Shape/Bill Pearl	$15.00	$
	Getting Stronger/Bill Pearl & Gary Moran	$19.00	$
	Nutrition Almanac/Nutrition Search	$15.95	$
	Kinesiology of Exercise/Dr. Yessis, Ph.D.	$17.95	$
	Secrets of Soviet Sports Fitness & Training/Dr. Yessis, Ph.D.	$12.95	$
	Body Shaping for Women/Dr. Yessis, Ph.D.	$16.95	$
	(Video) Exercise Mastery/Dr. Yessis, Ph.D.	$39.00	$
	(Video) Stretching/ Bob Anderson	$29.95	$
	(Video) Keys to Weight Training for Men & Women/Bill Pearl	$19.95	$
	Praise! Walk/Integrity Music (Each series contains 2 cassette tapes)		
	Beginner – Get Going & Taking Charge, Plus Free Hip Pack	$19.95	$
	Intermediate – Walk by Faith & Power Stride	$19.95	$
	Advanced – Walk This Way & Higher Power	$19.95	$

U.S. Funds Only. Add $2.50 postage & handling for the first item and $1.00 for each additional item. Wisconsin residents add 5% sales tax. For Priority Mail include an additional $2.00.

JBBA Publishing
P.O. Box 842
Appleton, WI 54912
1-800-245-7897

Name _____
Address _____
City/State/Zip _____
Telephone _____
VISA/MasterCard _____ Exp. _____

Allow 3-5 weeks. Satisfaction guaranteed or return for full refund.

Qty.	Title	Price	Total
	The Weight Training Workbook, 2nd Edition/Jim Bennett	$12.95	$
	The Weight Training Record, 2nd Edition/Jim Bennett	$10.95	$
	Getting in Shape/Bill Pearl	$15.00	$
	Getting Stronger/Bill Pearl & Gary Moran	$19.00	$
	Nutrition Almanac/Nutrition Search	$15.95	$
	Kinesiology of Exercise/Dr. Yessis, Ph.D.	$17.95	$
	Secrets of Soviet Sports Fitness & Training/Dr. Yessis, Ph.D.	$12.95	$
	Body Shaping for Women/Dr. Yessis, Ph.D.	$16.95	$
	(Video) Exercise Mastery/Dr. Yessis, Ph.D.	$39.00	$
	(Video) Stretching/ Bob Anderson	$29.95	$
	(Video) Keys to Weight Training for Men & Women/Bill Pearl	$19.95	$
	Praise! Walk/Integrity Music (Each series contains 2 cassette tapes)		
	Beginner – Get Going & Taking Charge, Plus Free Hip Pack	$19.95	$
	Intermediate – Walk by Faith & Power Stride	$19.95	$
	Advanced – Walk This Way & Higher Power	$19.95	$

U.S. Funds Only. Add $2.50 postage & handling for the first item and $1.00 for each additional item. Wisconsin residents add 5% sales tax. For Priority Mail include an additional $2.00.

JBBA Publishing
P.O. Box 842
Appleton, WI 54912
1-800-245-7897

Name _____
Address _____
City/State/Zip _____
Telephone _____
VISA/MasterCard _____ Exp. _____

Allow 3-5 weeks. Satisfaction guaranteed or return for full refund.